# The Truth About Northern Soul

## UNPACKING THE MYTHS

Stephen Riley

Aureus Publishing

First Published 2019
Digital Edition 2019

©2019   Stephen Riley
©2019   Digital Edition Stephen Riley
©2019   Digital Edition Aureus Publishing Limited

Stephen Riley has asserted the Author's right under the Copyright, Designs and Patents Act 1988 to be identified as Author of this Work.

All rights reserved.

Front cover: ©Stephen Riley.

ISBN 978-1-899750-45-0

Printed in Great Britain.

A catalogue record for this book is available from the British Library.

Aureus Publishing Limited

Tel: 00 44 (0) 1656 880033

E-mail:   sales@aureus.co.uk
Web site: www.aureus.co.uk

# CONTENTS

| | |
|---|---|
| Acknowledgements | 5 |
| A Note from the Author | 6 |
| What do I mean by Northern Soul's myths? | 8 |
| Everyone's gone to The Moon (if they couldn't get to the Wheel) | 12 |
| Just what is this Northern Soul 'genre' of music? | 33 |
| What is the appeal of Northern Soul? | 39 |
| When was Northern Soul? | 45 |
| Northern Soul was a response to the wretchedness of 70s working-class life, wasn't it? | 56 |
| There were no drugs, right? | 61 |
| There was no violence or bad behaviour; it was all sweetness and light, all S.O.U.L. – Sounds Of Unity and Love – wasn't it? | 69 |
| Everyone wore baggy pants and a bowling shirt, right? | 81 |
| You had to have sports bag…? | 87 |
| Everyone went round plastered in Northern Soul badges, didn't they? | 89 |
| Wigan Casino was the birth place of Northern Soul, wasn't it? | 91 |
| It was all about 60s music, wasn't it; none of that 70s music or that disco stuff? | 102 |
| Everybody was leaping about, doing backdrops and spins and that…. | 112 |
| Rarity, Divs and Handbaggers | 116 |
| Mouldy Oldies | 130 |
| Conclusion | 140 |
| Sources | 142 |
| Discography | 144 |

# Acknowledgements

Thanks to Fiona Scase for her patience and encouragement, to Kenny Lowe for remembering, reading and commenting, to Gillian Scott Moore for the photographs, to Pete Roberts for his permission to use shots of himself at the Twisted Wheel, and to the many anonymous individuals whose comments on social media helped shape this book.

Dedications
I dedicate this book to the memory of the following old soul boys; some I knew well, some were nodding acquaintances, some I loved like brothers:

William 'John' Seymour
Alan Seymour
Alan Mansfield
John Read
Neil Lomas
Neil Broadley
Ray Cowen
Greg Pollitt
Barry Lewin
Alf Hockaday
Billy Hockaday
Desi Rostron
Eric Ward

Gordon Thompson
John 'Dolly' Dolmor
Paul Craddock
Dave Griffith
Col Cocks
Charlie Briggs
Martyn Ellis
Mick Sayles
Vinnie Wathey
Sean O'Flaherty
Les Pyatt
Eldon Williams

## A Note from the Author

In recent years, Northern Soul has gone from being a small, marginal interest to a major cultural phenomenon. It has been appropriated into various forms of media and a great deal has been said and written about it. However, as someone who was part of the Northern Soul scene from way back – back, indeed, to before it was called 'Northern Soul' – much of what I hear and see written is wildly at odds with my own experience. I have therefore written this book in order to examine and counter some of the myths that now encumber the Northern Soul scene.

To give a few examples: there seem to be moves on the part of some to redefine the Northern Soul scene as some kind of drug-free, violence-free teenage utopia, or adolescents' Darby and Joan Club. That is very much not a true representation of the scene as I experienced it. The seldom challenged status of Wigan Casino as the scene's defining club is another aspect which is highly debatable and is challenged here. I also examine many of Northern Soul's stereotype images and symbols and ask if they are really representational of how people experienced the scene.

There are several books in circulation on Northern Soul, usually histories or personal memoirs. Although this book necessarily includes some of those aspects, they are asides, and its key driving force is a succession of popular Northern Soul myths, which I set out in order to examine and critique.

I see two main types of people enjoying this book: those who are new or relatively new to Northern Soul and would like to know more about the truth of its varied and not always edifying past, and those who, like me, have been around the block a few times and would appreciate a blunt, honest account of how things were, which echoes their own experiences.

Northern Soul has also now been recognised for the powerful cultural force that it was, and it has therefore, over the last few years, become the object of academic scrutiny. I hope that those who continue to research the subject will find this contribution a useful addition to the discussion.

As this book takes a hefty cattle-prod to many of Northern Soul's holy cows, I expect some people will find it controversial, and maybe some will even take offence. However, I hope that is not the case and that all who read it will appreciate it for its candour and will recognise that popularised beliefs are not necessarily truths and that the Northern Soul scene is not well served if it is represented by misleading parodies. I further hope that readers will recognise that this book is not meant to be critical of Northern Soul, overall, even if it highlights aspects some will see as negative. This is because many of the things seen as negatives at this critical distance were part of what made the scene attractive to those on the scene at the time. It is, however, critical of certain musical blind-alleys followed at times and of other dubious, extraneous things that have attached themselves to the scene. I therefore hope that this book negates some negatives and gives a true account, warts and all, of a profoundly vibrant and influential club and music scene.

# What do I mean by Northern Soul's myths?

In September 2013 the Tory Party conference was about to get under way in Manchester. In seeking something pithy and topical to say about this fairly lumpen piece of news, that great authority on working-class culture, The Telegraph, announced that this was also the fortieth anniversary of the opening of Wigan Casino and, with that, 'the birth of Northern Soul'[1]. The newspaper then used this meaningless coincidence to say that what the Tories needed was to find their 'Northern Soul' (dodgy pun intended); i.e.: to re-engage with the sensibilities of northern people, alienated by London/wealth-centric politics.

This book is not concerned with the Tories or the Telegraph's advice to them; what it is concerned with are the popular myths which surround Northern Soul. The conflation of Wigan Casino and Northern Soul, the belief that Wigan Casino and Northern Soul were coincident and maybe even more or less one and the same thing is one of the key myths. The truth is that Northern Soul had been around for many years before Wigan Casino opened. It is misleading beliefs such as this that this book is intended to challenge.

Wrong and revisionist histories have been applied to the Northern Soul scene with seemingly greater intensity over the last few years, and palpable ignorance and misunderstandings have become more noticeable. Whereas this phenomenon is often apparent in comments and attitudes heard live on the scene and in various traditional forms of commentary, like newspapers and television shows, it is the opening up to all of the right to be heard via internet sites that has been most revealing. A recent post on Facebook, in which the writer had noticed a similarity between Motown and Northern Soul and asked others if they had also spotted this resemblance, is indicative. The Motown sound and Northern Soul are intrinsically linked. The Northern Soul scene always played some Motown records, and many non-Motown records

---

[1] Hardman, Isabel. 26 Sept. 2013. Tories are searching for their Northern Soul. The Telegraph [online] Available: http://www.telegraph.co.uk/news/politics/conservative/10336844/Tories-are-searching-for-their-northern-Soul.html [Accessed 29 May 2016]

played on the scene clearly carry more than a hint of the Motown sound, such was the power and influence of that label in the 1960s when most of the music we now called 'Northern Soul' was recorded. The record many would think of as the definitive Northern Soul record, Frank Wilson's 'Do I love You', is a Motown record. Of course, much of this can be dismissed as forgivable ignorance on the part of newcomers to the scene. However, there are much more prescriptive and dogmatic interventions.

One can now purchase 'Northern Soul dance lessons', as though it is a particular form, like any of various strict traditional dance styles – a matter which would come as a great surprise to the tens of thousands of Soul/Northern Soul fans who have been dancing to this music in their own ways for decades.

At times, commentary, at the same time as being ill-informed or wilfully misleading, becomes aggressive and boorish. The following is an example and an indicator of how myths are created and held in place. In a recent social media post, someone called another person a 'plank' for suggesting that Elvis Presley's 'Rubberneckin'' had been played at The Twisted Wheel, on account of the 'fact' that said record "wasn't released until 1973 and The Wheel closed in 1971". In point of fact, 'Rubberneckin'' was recorded and released in 1969 – a piece of information available from many sources to anyone with internet access – plus the record was well-known on the Northern Soul scene in around 1971-72.

Whether or not it was played specifically at The Wheel is dubious, and my efforts to clear the matter up decisively only provoked more of the same bluster and myth-making: I asked on one of Facebook's Twisted Wheel sites whether any veteran Wheelers remembered the record being played. My question attracted a mixture of helpful remarks and derision. One of the most eye-catching comments came from an individual who seemed outraged that anyone should even dare ask such a thing, or associate a non-Soul act like Presley with the hallowed establishment.

His comments were framed in the kind of tone one might expect from the BBC, if someone insulted The Queen. In pious indignation, he pointed out that the revered venue never played anything but "classic pure Soul". It was "an insult" and "sacrilege" to suggest Presley's music was in any way associated with The Wheel. If his comments were not risible enough for their pompous tone, their total inaccuracy completed the job.

For one thing, there seems a broad consensus that Presley's 'Mystery Train' was played at The Wheel, back in its early, Brazennose Street, days; for another, The Wheel is well known, over its whole lifespan, to have played a huge amount of non-Soul: Blues, RnB, Reggae, Ska and Bluebeat, and a good deal of music by white performers, which might in other contexts be seen as Rock, Pop or even Cajun/Country. Some of the club's most memorable (and forgettable) record spins were by white acts: Mitch Ryder, Ronnie Milsap, Mickey Lee Lane, The Human Beinz, The Castaways, Charlie Rich, Wayne Fontana, Andre Brasseur, The Mood Mosaic (Mark P. Wirtz) featuring the Ladybirds, The Dynatones, The Blendells, P J Proby and Tony Joe White, to name but a few; and if Wikipedia is to be trusted, 'Na Na Hey Hey Kiss Him Goodbye' by Steam – a pretty iffy pop record and one, one would have thought, even further down the credibility food-chain than Presley's 'Rubberneckin' – was also played[2].

Many of the venue's live acts were white, including The Spencer Davis Group, John Mayall, Long John Baldry, Julie Driscoll and the Brian Auger Trinity, Zoot Money, Georgie Fame, The Alan Bown Set, The Mike Cotton Sound, The Action and The Amboy Dukes. It is hard to see this individual's comments as anything more than a desire to hold in place a nostalgic reinvention of the club as a "pure", Soul-only venue, when it was clearly not[3]. One can only speculate on his motivations, though one must suspect that as the scene came to identify itself as solely a Soul scene – though that was never entirely true of it at any point in its history – and Soul is seen in this milieu to have more kudos than other musical forms, the historical facts have to be bent to fit the myth – and to be supported with as much bluster as possible. The bullying that took place in the thread that followed my question resulted in one person leaving the group and with me wondering, even if 'Rubberneckin'' had been played, anyone would dare say so.

I say these things not to impugn the reputation of clubs like the Wheel, but to make the point that the Mod scene encompassed a broad spectrum of music, and when the Northern Soul scene emerged, it took some of that baggage along for the ride too, in spite of it having the word 'Soul' now firmly attached to it, with all the expectations that suggests.

Another troubling aspect of a wide and varied range of distortions has been the attempt by some to impose retrospectively-invented 'rules'. Attempts to fit Northern Soul into arbitrary, self-styled boxes proliferate, often by people who arrived on the scene at the end of or after its heyday. This book is an attempt not only to set things straight, but to give the scene chance to breathe again, outside of the various rules that some individuals seem to need to

---

[2] Wikipedia [online] Twisted Wheel Club Available: https://en.wikipedia.org/wiki/Twisted_Wheel_Club [Accessed 9 January 2018]
[3] I should add that when I responded to this the commentator's remarks and pointed out these contradictions, he redacted the word 'pure', leaving just 'classic soul'.

apply to it via retrospective reinventions of the Northern Soul scene's history.

It would seem necessary to say a bit about my credentials to speak in this regard, for three reasons: firstly, much of what you see here comes from empirical research, the source of which is my own first-hand experience, which often differs from the myths and therefore needs setting out. I should add, however, that there is also a good deal of further research to investigate issues and back-up points made. Secondly, because the first thing you hear when you stick your head above the parapet to speak on this subject is 'who are you to talk?', or more expressive words to the same effect – people want to know who you are, where you went, and when, before they decide how to react to what you have to say. Thirdly, there is nothing remarkable about my experience and, in its routine-ness, it becomes a useful archetype. Having heard pivotal figures like Ady Croasdell, Ian Levine and many less well-known people talk about their first exposure to Soul, I see my early experience as largely the same and therefore a useful exemplar, both because of its typicality and because that time was more or less the moment when a more varied Soul scene mutated into the one we now know as 'Northern Soul'.

Whilst acknowledging those who were around sooner and made the transition from the mod scene of the mid-60s through to what I am talking about here, the pattern usually goes something like this: exposed to Motown by friends or older siblings or the local youth club toward the end of the 1960s; attends local Soul/ proto-Northern Soul club (the term Northern Soul was not in use then), listening to Motown, Ska, Bluebeat, Reggae and what will eventually get the epithet 'Northern Soul'; moves up to proper night clubs that play music that forms the basis of what will come to be called the Northern Soul scene. For these reasons, I feel my introduction to this music and scene is worth summarising, and I hope readers will forgive some personal reflections, which are used as a platform from which to move into more objective observations.

With that said, what this book is not is another reworking of the 'story of Northern Soul': the well-known tale of a Mod scene that refused to die, the playing-out of the better known records, the pursuit of rare imported discs, enthusiasts' record-collecting trips to America, Dave Godin's accidental labelling of the scene and so on. Although these will be touched on in context, they are matters well covered elsewhere. What this book is about, therefore, is the experience of the scene from someone who was in it as one of the ordinary grunts on the ground; not a DJ, promoter, major record collector, or celebrity bandwagon-jumper who happened to grow up within fifty miles of Wigan and gets wheeled out to repeat the same old second-hand knowledge every time there is another Northern Soul revival.

# Everyone's gone to The Moon (if they couldn't get to the Wheel)

I got very lucky: I lived in Stalybridge, which straddles the River Tame on the eastern edge of what would later become Greater Manchester. Growing up in Stalybridge is not something normally associated with the term 'lucky'. It was a hard-up, worn-out mill town, still in unfashionable, broke, north-east Cheshire, then; the bit that got amputated just below Stockport in 1974, when the boundaries were redrawn, relieving the fine folk of Knutsford, Alderley Edge, Wilmslow and the rest of county's affluent enclaves of that uncomfortable association. On a plateau overlooking Stalybridge was Dukinfield, which was more or less another Stalybridge, but with whatever charm its valley-dwelling neighbour had extracted. What Dukinfield did have going for it, however, was a nightclub called 'The Moon'. Its DJs, names that were bandied about at the time included Al Ford, Al Devine and Mark Anthony, were aficionados of Manchester's Twisted Wheel and brought the same playlists to this local venue. The Moon was within walking distance of my house.

My first trip to The Moon was in 1969. At just fourteen, I was far too young to get in officially, and only did so because my mate, Simeon's, dad and big brother were bouncers[4]. We were dragged along with the men to give our mothers an hour or so's evening peace and quiet. Our token task was to carry in trays of muffins for the snack bar, and then be out of sight and out of mind for a bit. This was fine by us; we handed over the muffins, then slunk away quietly into the darkness to spin-out the experience as long as possible.

To someone who had never been in a night club and had probably never even contemplated the existence of such things till now, the place was out of this world - almost literally. Following the theme the name suggested, it was decked out like The Moon's surface. The dance floor was made from riveted

---

[4] Simeon Stafford; his dad and brother were Fred and Barry. Fred would later become the manager of The Moon.

sheet steel and surrounded by seating places fashioned from silver-painted concrete, moulded over chicken wire to look like craters, with an eruption in the middle to form a kind of table to put your drinks on. To complete the image, the DJ's booth was a mock Moon landing craft. The space was very dark and what little light there was came from ultra violet lights, which made it very mysterious and exotic to my unworldly eyes. Periodically, a strobe would kick in, throwing rapid-fire light onto the dancers. Figures burst from black invisibility into blinding light in fractions of a second; shirts, miniskirts and white tights juddered; each frozen moment a split-second still in a jerky, black-and-white movie.

*The Moon Club, Dukinfield, now in Greater Manchester, early 1970s. Picture source unknown. Judging by the flyers for a 'folk night' and the faded club name, it had probably closed by this stage. It ran from around 1969 to 1972. Prior to that it was The Oxford Cinema. After it ceased to be The Moon it stood empty for a while before reopening as Hiccups disco, and later as Drifters disco. It was demolished and replaced by a Morrisons supermarket in 1981. The supermarket's petrol station now occupies this spot.*

Even entering The Moon was an experience. After passing through the main entrance and paying at the till, you crossed the foyer to heavy inner double doors, which opened onto a large metal cylinder, which was the corridor into the dark velvety space of the club's main room. As I heaved those doors open for the first time and stepped into the giant galvanised tube, the Isley Brothers' 'Behind a Painted Smile' kicked off at immense volume. The effect was electrifying. The mysterious smells and sights of the place itself coupled with that powerful music, with its wistful beginning blasting-off into crashing drums and soaring vocals, had an emotional impact beyond anything had experienced before, beyond even what I had ever thought was possible. I was hooked.

The only context in which I had encountered the term 'soul' at that time was in Religious Education classes at school. The fact that it was also a form of music was, up to that point, something that was completely unknown to me, even if I had heard one or two hit Soul records on the radio without knowing they were called that. It seems strange now to recall that there were no commercial radio stations then, that the BBC more or less owned musical broadcasting, and there was no legal pop music station in Britain until late in 1967, when Radio One came into existence. During some of Soul's most productive years the only official radio outlet for popular music in the UK was BBC's Light Programme, and, of what the BBC deemed 'light music', only a proportion was pop/rock/Soul. There were, however, pirate radio stations and TV programmes, like Ready, Steady, Go, so major acts like the Four Tops, Otis Redding and the Temptations did enjoy some exposure and UK success. But it is also telling that many of the records that I and many other Soul fans would come to realise were originally by black American artists met our ears first as cover versions by white Brits. Lulu had a big UK hit with 'Shout'; the Isley Brothers, who also did it, and wrote it, did not. The Searchers had a big UK hit with 'Sweets for My Sweet'; the Drifters, who also recorded it, did not. The Hollies had a big UK hit with 'Just One Look'; Doris Troy, who co-wrote it and performed it, did not. Herman's Hermits had a big UK hit with 'I'm Into Something Good'; Earl Jean's original is more or less unknown. And on it goes. Tracks such as 'There's Always Something There to Remind Me', 'Anyone Who Had a Heart', 'Twist and Shout', 'Mr Postman', 'You Really Got a Hold on Me' and many more were very familiar to young British music lovers and a lay public, but only as cover versions – the original black American recordings remained largely unheard.

My Moon experience was repeated perhaps another couple of times in 1969 before my friendship with Simeon drifted, as teenage friendships often do. It was then difficult to get into The Moon again, fourteen years old, muffinless and with the wrong clothes, so I made the best of things at nearby St. Johns youth club, where some of the marginally older lads would bring in their Stax, Chess, Atlantic and Motown records. By the end of the year I'd bought my own first few discs: 'Jimmy Mack', with 'Third Finger Left Hand' on the B-side, by Martha Reeves and the Vandellas; 'The Return of Django' by the

Upsetters; and the LP 'British Motown Chartbusters Volume 2'. It is an aspect of the scene repeated in many places at that time that what would become Northern Soul was mixed with Ska, Bluebeat and Reggae.

I had also resolved to collect every Tamla Motown record ever released. I believe Ian Levine had the same ambition at about the same time. Being of a different income bracket, he may have achieved it; I did not.

By 1970, paper-round tips had bought me what were briefly the right clothes – rolled-up Levis, Jaytex button-down collar shirt, braces and (believe it or not) hobnailed boots – and I managed to blag my way into The Moon, again, regardless of the fact that I would only turn fifteen in the middle of the year. Hobnailed boots were, incidentally, soon banned at The Moon because of their devastating effects during the many fights, and Dr Martens became the boot of choice.

The Twisted Wheel was much talked about by older lads and took on a kind of mystical quality. It was the 'Mecca', the place you had to go to. I, however, was too young and skint for the bright lights of central Manchester. Maddeningly, just as I started work in 1971 and had a few bob in my pocket for the first time, The Wheel closed. But for the time being, The Moon was not a bad compromise. Plus, there were other clubs out in the sticks at the same time which would also play some Soul: The Birdcage in Ashton-under-Lyne, The Bower Club in Stalybridge and The Crystal in Glossop.

The following is a list of what you could hear at that time in these clubs and on collectors' turntables. I make a point of listing so many because of the associated myths: the belief on the part of many that these records first materialised at Wigan Casino. I recently heard a DJ spin Andre Brasseur's 'The Kid' and call it a 'Wigan classic'. Elsewhere – on Facebook – one punter called another an 'idiot' for suggesting 'There's Nothing Else to Say' by the Incredibles had a life before Mr M's.

(Mr M's, for the uninitiated, was a disco within a disco at Wigan Casino; a smaller room, upstairs and off the main one, which specialised in what were oldies even then.)

I will also pick out certain tracks that have particular significance as turning points in the development of the Northern Soul scene, as we came to know it.

The following are most of what I can recall at the time of writing. Most would have been heard at The Moon, The Twisted Wheel and various other similarly-minded clubs in the period I am describing: 1969 to 1971, when The Wheel closed. The Moon closed not long afterwards. I know I am missing many; for every track listed there are many that are not. No doubt people will be screaming at the page: "what about....??!!". But a list like this could never be exhaustive and, were it complete, this would be a very long chapter, but it gives a flavour and it captures the most significant tracks. Certainly many Motown records will be missing. Should I, for example, have included 'Cleo's Mood' and 'Cleo's Back' by Junior Walker and the All Stars? These were certainly tracks that would have been known to most Soul aficionados at the time, and they got spins on my and my mates' turntables, but their pace probably places them in the period before that under discussion here, in terms of their actually being spun in clubs. Northern Soul might not yet have acquired its specific identity, but a clear preference for faster tracks had become established. Similarly, there could be more Chess, Checker and Cadet records, but by 1969 many of the more R&B-ish sounding tracks that these sister labels are best known for would have fallen out of favour. So, what I hope I have done is to list most of the tracks from around then which have continued to be played on the scene. I should also be abundantly clear that many of these records I mention had been around for some time when I first heard them – some from when they were first released, others from the late 60s, as enthusiasts discovered them. I do not want to fall foul of the 'when I first heard it equals when it was first played' folly. The many mid-60s Mod clubs, scattered across the UK, would have been familiar with a lot of these records. Let's just say, it was at least these tracks that were around at the time.

Reflecting the sexual politics of the era – The Female Eunuch was only just published (1970)[5] and had yet to gain currency – you would hear lots of 'girlie' records, chosen to keep the girls on the dance floor, to make the place look busy early on and to keep the lads interested, tracks such as:

Da Doo Ron Ron – The Crystals
Be My Baby; (The Best Part of) Breakin' Up – The Ronettes
Chapel of Love – The Dixie Cups
Sweet Talking Guy; Out of this World; Keep the Boy Happy – The Chiffons
My Guy; What's Easy for Two is So Hard for One – Mary Wells
Reaching for Something I Can't Have; When You're Young and in Love – The Marvelettes
The Clapping Song – Shirley Ellis
My Boyfriend's Back – The Angels
The Locomotion – Little Eva
Jimmy Mack; Third Finger Left Hand – Martha Reeves and the Vandellas
Needle in a Haystack; He Was Really Saying Something – The Velvelettes

[5] Greer, Germaine. The Female Eunuch (1970) Edition: Harper Perennial Classics, New York, 2006

Baby Love; Where Did Our Love Go – The Supremes
It's in His Kiss – Betty Everett
It Takes Two – Marvin Gaye and Kim Weston
Two Can Have a Party; The Onion Song – Marvin Gaye and Tammi Terrell

You would also hear danceable Soul records that were well known amongst a more general public, and in some cases had even charted, such as:

Seven Days Too Long – Chuck Wood
Ain't Nothing but a House Party – The Showstoppers
Dance to the Music – Sly and the Family Stone
Higher and Higher – Jackie Wilson
Saturday Night at the Movies; Under the Boardwalk; At the Club – The Drifters
Another Saturday Night; Twisting the Night Away – Sam Cooke
Stop Her on Sight (SOS); Headline News – Edwin Starr
Harlem Shuffle – Bob and Earl
Papa's Got a Brand New Bag – James Brown and the Famous Flames
I Feel Love Comin' On – Felice Taylor
Sitting on the Dock of the Bay – Otis Redding
A Lover's Concerto – the Toys
1,2,3; Like a Baby – Len Barry
Rescue Me – Fontella Bass
Nothing But a Heartache – The Flirtations
The In Crowd – Dobie Gray

And there was a lot of well-known Tamla Motown music. Indeed, no other label is anywhere near as well-represented as Tamla Motown in this stage of Northern Soul's genealogy. In addition to those I have categorised in other ways above and below, the following well-known Tamla Motown tracks were commonplace:

I Can't Help Myself; Standing in the Shadows of Love; Reach Out I'll be There – The Four Tops
Roadrunner; How Sweet It Is – Jr Walker and the All Stars
Get Ready; Ain't Too Proud to Beg – The Temptations
Dancing in the Street; Nowhere to Run – Martha Reeves and the Vandellas
Uptight; I Was Made to Love Her – Stevie Wonder
Put Yourself in My Place; I Guess I'll Always Love You; Behind a Painted Smile – The Isley Brothers
Put Yourself in My Place; Heaven Must Have Sent You – The Elgins
Twenty Five Miles – Edwin Starr
I Heard it Through the Grapevine; Too Busy Thinking About My Baby;

Wherever I Lay My Hat – Marvin Gaye
I Miss You Baby (How I Miss You) – Marv Johnson
Just a Little Misunderstanding; First I Look at the Purse – The Contours
What Becomes of the Brokenhearted; I've Passed This Way Before; I'll Say Forever My Love – Jimmy Ruffin
I Second that Emotion; The Tracks of My Tears; Tears of a Clown – Smokey Robinson and the Miracles

There was also loads of well-known Stax and Atlantic stuff:

Soul Man; I Thank You; You Don't know Like I know; Soul Sister Brown Sugar; Hold on I'm Coming; Soothe Me – Sam and Dave
Last Night – The Mar-Keys
Green Onions – Booker T and the MGs
Love Man; Shake; I Can't Turn You Loose; Hard to Handle; Satisfaction; Respect - Otis Redding
Soul Finger – Bar-Kays
Who's Making Love – Johnny Taylor
Land of 1,000 Dances; 634-5789; Mustang Sally; Three Time Loser; In the Midnight Hour – Wilson Pickett
Funky Street; Sweet Soul Music – Arthur Conley
Sock It to 'em JB – Rex Garvin and the Mighty Cravers
Show Me – Joe Tex
Private Number – Judy Clay and William Bell
See Saw – Don Covay and the Goodtimers

And then there was the other stuff, the sort of music that would be less known or unknown outside of the clubs, at that time. Most of this has now been accepted into the Northern Soul canon, as indeed have most of the records mentioned above. Within this list, there is still plenty of Motown, Stax and Atlantic, but it is of a more, or at least slightly more, obscure bent, or, at least, it was at the time – many of these tracks, particularly the Motown ones, have become well known to a more general listenership since:

Sho Nuff Got a Good Thing; But it's Alright – J J Jackson
I'll Do Anything – Doris Troy
Lay This Burden Down – Mary Love
Picture Me Gone – Evie Sands
The Beat; Um Um Um Um Um; Monkey Time; Ain't No Soul (in These Old Shoes) – Major Lance
We're in this Thing Together – The Carrolls[6]
Mr. Soul – Bud Harper

---
[6] And no doubt the Peaches and Herb version too, but it's the Carrolls one that I remember.

In the Midnight Hour – Little Mac and the Boss Sounds
Baby Help Me – Percy Sledge
I Can't Get a Hold of Myself – Clifford Curry
Our Love Will Grow – Norman Johnson and the Showmen
Let the Good Times Roll and Feel So Good – Bunny Sigler
There's No Stopping Us Now – Diana Ross and the Supremes
Candy to Me – Eddie Holland
Shotgun; Shake and Fingerpop – Junior Walker and the All Stars
Some Kind of Wonderful – Soul Brothers Six
Little Piece of Leather[7] – Donnie Elbert
Karate Boogaloo – Jerryo
Little Darling – Marvin Gaye
60 Minutes of Your Love – Homer Banks
I Spy for the FBI – Jamo Thomas and His Party Brothers Orchestra
Helpless – Kim Weston
Don't Tell Your Mama; Bring it on Home to Me; Things Get Better – Eddie Floyd
Keep on Loving Me – Frances Nero
Hole in the Wall; Go Head On – The Packers
I've Got a Feeling – Barbara Randolph
I've Got a Feeling – The Isley Brothers
I'll Always Love You – The Detroit Spinners
Way Over There; My Weakness is You; I Want My Baby Back – Edwin Starr
I Gotta Let You Go – Martha Reeves and the Vandellas
Girl, Why You Wanna Make Me Blue; The Way You Do the Things You Do; You're Not an Ordinary Girl; Beauty's Only Skin Deep – The Temptations
Something About You; Since You've Been Gone; Shake Me Wake Me; Without the One You Love – The Four Tops
It's So Hard Being a Loser – The Contours
Just Walk in My Shoes – Gladys Knight and the Pips
These Things Will Keep Me Loving You – The Velvelettes
Baby What I Mean – The Drifters
Our Love is in the Pocket; Open the Door to Your Heart – Darrell Banks
The Kid – Andre Brasseur
Billy's Bag – Billy Preston
Freedom Train; That's What I Want to Know – James Carr
Cool Jerk – The Three Caps (AKA The Capitols)
Boogaloo Party – The Flamingos
Comin' Home Baby – Mel Torme
The 81 – Candy and the Kisses
The Boy from New York City – The Ad-Libs
The Horse – Cliff Nobles and Co.

---
[7] The original, Sue label version, not that dodgy early-70s reworking.

Be Young Be Foolish Be Happy – The Tams
Lickin' Stick – George Torrence
Pata Pata – Miriam Makeba
Love is After Me – Charlie Rich
Getting Mighty Crowded – Betty Everett
Hold On – The Radiants
Crazy 'Bout You Baby; Dust My Broom – Ike and Tina Turner
Let's Go Baby (Where the Action is); Barefootin' – Robert Parker
Mr Bang Bang Man – Little Hank
Polk Salad Annie – Tony Joe White
She's Looking Good – Roger Collins
Little Ole Man (Uptight – Everything's Alright) – Bill Cosby
I Got What It Takes – Brooks and Jerry
Bring Your Love Back to Me – Linda Lyndell
The Who Who Song – Jackie Wilson
What's Wrong with Me Baby – The Invitations
I'm Gonna Miss You; Hope We Have – The Artistics
Fife Piper – The Dynatones
Baby Do the Philly Dog; Mine Exclusively – The Olympics
Everybody's Going to a Love In – Bob Brady and the ConChords
That Driving Beat; Secret Home – Willie Mitchell
Washed Ashore; With this Ring; Sweet Sweet Loving – The Platters
Get Out of My Heart; My Illusive Dreams – Moses and Joshua
Earthquake – Al 'TNT' Braggs
Devil with a Blue Dress On/Good Golly Miss Molly; Breakout – Mitch Ryder and the Detroit Wheels
Friday Night – Johnny Taylor
Behind Locked Doors – Witches and the Warlock
I Feel So Bad – Jackie Edwards
Let's Copp a Groove – Bobby Wells
There's Nothing Else to Say – The Incredibles
At the Discotheque; Everything's Wrong – Chubby Checker
Ain't that Terrible – The Capitols
She Blew a Good Thing – The Poets
Going to a Happening – Tommy Neal
The Cheater – Bob Kuban and the In Men
I Can't Satisfy; You've Been Cheating; Amen – The Impressions[8]
Help Me; Chain Reaction – The Spellbinders
Twine Time; Philly Freeze – Alvin Cash
Let Love Come Between Us; Shake a Tail Feather; Do Unto Me – James and Bobby Purify

---

[8] In truth, I cannot remember which version of 'Amen' was played – The Impressions or Otis Redding. Quite possibly both got a spin.

A Touch of Velvet – A Sting of Brass – The Mood Mosiac
Soul Serenade – Mike Cotton Sound[9]
6 by 6 – Earl van Dyke and the Motown Brass
I Can't Help Myself (Sugar Pie, Honey Bunch) – Earl van Dyke and the Soul Brothers
Love Makes a Woman; Am I the Same Girl – Barbara Acklin
Wade in the Water – Ramsey Lewis Trio
Soulful Dress – Sugar Pie DeSanto
Wang Dang Doodle – Ko Ko Taylor
Recovery – Fontella Bass
Nothing Can Stop Me – Gene Chandler
The Right Track – Billy Butler
Girls are Out to Get You – The Fascinations
Moody Woman – Jerry Butler
The Duck – Jackie Lee
Soul Time – Shirley Ellis
Sweet Happiness – Newby and Johnson
Dance With Me; La La La La La – The Blendells
Never Love a Robin – Barbara and Brenda
That's What Love is Made Of – The Miracles[10]
That's Enough – Roscoe Robinson
Train, Keep on Movin' – 5th Dimension
Get on Up; And Get Away – The Esquires
I Can't Make It (Without You baby) – Bessie Banks
Liar Liar – The Castaways
Candy – The Astors
Keep on Talking – James Barnett
I Can't Turn You Loose – The Chambers Brothers
Sock it to 'Em Soul Brother – Bill Moss
Earthquake – Bobbi Lynn
Sign on the Dotted Line – Gene Latter
Trampoline – The Spencer Davis Group
I Got the Fever – The Prophets (AKA Creation)
Competition Ain't Nothin' – Little Carl Carlton
Love on a Mountain Top – Robert Knight
Don't Leave Me – Al Greene and the Soul Mates
Green Door – Wynder K Frog
A Little Bit Hurt – Julien Covey and The Machine
Who's Fooling Who – The Amboy Dukes

---

[9] It may have been this version I heard, it could equally have been the Beau Dollar and the Coins version – both were played.
[10] As in 'Smokey Robinson and the Miracles', but at the time of that recording he was not given separate billing.

Time is Tight – Booker T and the MGs
Black Pearl – Sonny Charles and the Checkmates Ltd
Shine it On – Vernon Garrett
Treat Her Right – Roy Head
Mellow Moonlight – Roy Docker with Music Through Six
Your Eyes May Shine – The Short Kuts featuring Eddie Harrison
Oh How Happy – Shades of Blue
Apples Peaches Pumpkin Pie; Baby Make Your Own Sweet Music – Jay and the Techniques
Stay Close to Me – Five Stairsteps and Cubie
Working on Your Case – The O'Jays
Girl Watcher – The O'Kaysions
Happy – William Bell
Shoes; Call on Me – Bobby Bland
Shotgun Wedding – Roy C

Bluebeat, Ska and Reggae were part of the scene too. The following tracks were amongst those played:

The Israelites; It Mek – Desmond Dekker
Reggae in Your Jeggae – Dandy
Wet Dream – Max Romeo
Guns of Navarone – The Skatalites
Al Capone; Ten Commandments of Man; Wreck a Pum Pum – Prince Buster
Wreck a Buddy – The Soul Sisters
Vietnam – Jimmy Cliff
Return of Django – Upsetters
Liquidator – Harry J All Stars
Skinhead Moonstomp – Symarip
Elizabethan Reggae – Boris Gardner
Phoenix City – Roland Alphonso

There was quite a bit of pop/rock played too, albeit generally of an R&B bent. The playing of these in relation to what we might think of them now is an interesting issue, about which I will say more below.

Opus 17(Don't You Worry About Me); Sherry; Working My Way Back to You – The Four Seasons
Groovin with Mr Bloe – Mr Bloe
Woolly Bully; Ring Dang Doo – Sam the Sham and the Pharaohs
Bread and Butter; Run Baby Run – The Newbeats
Hang on Sloopy – The McCoys
Let's Dance – Chris Montez

Mony Mony – Tommy James and the Shondells
Quick Joey Small – Kasenetz-Katz Singing Orchestral Circus
Na Na Hey Hey Kiss Him Goodbye - Steam
Spirit in the Sky – Norman Greenbaum
Black Skin Blue Eyed Boys – The Equals
Sultana – Titanic
Are You Ready – Pacific Gas and Electric
Something Keeps Calling Me Back – Wayne Fontana
Nikki Hoeky – P J Proby

The process of actively seeking overlooked records, by those with the resources that made that possible, was now well under way, and a large amount of music new to the scene, if recorded some years earlier, had started to appear. In particular, but by no means exclusively, Mirwood, Okeh and Ric Tic catalogues were being mined. As things moved on, the UK-based Mojo record label came into existence and started to re-issue a good deal of what had previously been obscure. The Contempo label would be created and do likewise a couple of years later. Existing labels, Jay Boy and President, did similar, as did Tamla Motown, Probe, Bell, United Artists and others. Bootlegging was also well under way by 1971, and songs circulated as 'pressings' or phoney imports. Genuine imports also became more easily available. By these various means, recent discoveries and records that had been around for some time but until now had been too rare for most to get their hands on had started to become accessible. This selection, now no doubt known to most on the scene as Northern Soul standards, were by this point reasonably easy to find and were regular club spins or even passé:

Tightrope – Inez and Charlie Foxx
Talk of the Grapevine – Donald Height
I Get the Sweetest Feeling – Jackie Wilson
Hey Girl Don't Bother Me; Silly Little Girl – The Tams
Let's Wade in the Water – Marlena Shaw
Makin' Up Time – The Holidays
This Thing Called Love – Johnny Wyatt
Back Street; Agent Double-O-Soul – Edwin Starr
The Matador; You Don't Want Me No More – Major Lance
Please Let Me In; Real Humdinger – J J Barnes
You've Got to Pay the Price; Ooh Pretty Lady – Al Kent
You've Got to Pay the Price – Gloria Taylor
Baby Reconsider – Leon Haywood
I'm Gonna Run Away From You – Tammi Lynn
One Wonderful Moment – The Shakers
Nothing Worse than Being Alone – The Ad Libs

Sweet and Easy – Van McCoy Strings
You Get Your Kicks – Mitch Ryder and The Detroit Wheels
Gonna Fix You Good – Little Anthony and the Imperials
I Want – Errol Dixon
Ready, Willing and Able – Jimmy Holiday and Clydie King
Nobody But Me – The Human Beinz
There Was a Time – Gene Chandler
Kick That Little Foot Sally Ann – Round Robin
A Lil' Lovin' Sometimes – Alexander Patton
Chains of Love; Good Things Come to Those Who Wait – Chuck Jackson
Determination; Tell Her – Dean Parrish
Same Old Thing – The Olympics
We're in This Thing Together – Peaches and Herb
You Turned My Bitter Into Sweet – Mary Love
Someday We're Gonna Love Again – Barbara Lewis
Good Time Tonight – The Soul Sisters
Hooked by Love – Homer Banks
Restless – Margie Hendrix
Dr. Love – Bobby Sheen
Ain't No Soul (Left in These Old Shoes) – Ronnie Milsap
Out on the Floor – Dobie Gray
Chills and Fever – Paul Kelly
Keep Saying (You Don't Love Nobody) – Charles Wright
Free for All – Phillip Mitchell
Backfield in Motion – Mel and Tim
Next in Line – Hoagy Lands
Walking Up a One Way Street – Willie Tee
From The Teacher to the Preacher – Gene Chandler and Barbara Acklin
Gotta Draw the Line – Darrow Fletcher
All for You – Earl van Dyke and the Soul Brothers Orchestra
Cigarette Ashes – Jimmy Conwell
That Beatin Rhythm – Richard Temple
Oh My Darling; Do the Temptation Walk; Darkest Days; Shotgun and the Duck – Jackie Lee
Humphrey Stomp – Earl Harrison
Love Love Love – Bobby Hebb
A Love You Can Depend On – Brenda and the Tabulations
Bar-B-Q – Wendy Rene
More More More of Your Love – Bob Brady and the ConChords
All Turned On – Bob Wilson and the San Remo Strings
Festival Time – The San Remo Strings
To Win Your Heart – Laura Lee
At the Top of the Stairs – The Formations

Gotta Have Your Love – The Sapphires
Wade in the Water – Sonny Stitt
You're Ready Now – Frankie Valli
I Feel an Urge Coming On – Jo Armstead
You're Gonna Make Me Love You – Sandi Sheldon
Too Late; A Quitter Never Wins – Larry Williams and Johnny Watson
I Don't Want to Discuss It; A Little Bit of Something (Beats a Whole Lot of Nothing); Poor Dog – Little Richard

There were also new releases that were played at the time:

Friendship Train – Gladys Knight and the Pips
Cloud Nine; I Can't Get Next to You – Temptations
Kool and the Gang – Kool and the Gang
Lunar Funk – The Fabulous Counts
What Does it Take – Jr Walker and the All Stars
Band of Gold; Deeper and Deeper; Rock Me in the Cradle (of Your Lovin' Arms) – Freda Payne
Give Me Just a Little More Time; You've Got Me Dangling on a String; Everything's Tuesday – Chairmen of the Board
Westbound Number Nine – The Flaming Ember
Somebody's Been Sleeping – 100 Proof Aged in Soul
While You're Out Looking for Sugar – The Honey Cone
Time; War – Edwin Starr
Get Up I Feel Like Being a Sex Machine; Hey America – James Brown
Sang and Dance – The Bar-Kays
Why Don't You Love Me – John Miles
Get Ready for Love – Paintbox
Move on Up – Curtis Mayfield

Looking at the above, particularly when considering the categories I have slotted things into, immediately highlights anomalies and myths. Some of these records are 'pop' records, whilst some are (Northern) Soul records, but often the distinction seems arbitrary. What I've called pop/rock might for others be Northern Soul; some that I have listed as Northern Soul others would call 'pop'.

In the late 60s to early 70s mail-order record sellers would often list 'Soul' and 'Motown' as discrete categories, indicating that these were considered similar but separate things. For many fans of slower, deeper Soul, Motown and much Northern Soul was and would still be regarded as too lightweight to be considered 'Soul' at all. Motown, so the story goes, was Berry Gordy's attempt to bring black American music to a broader audience by melding it with the softer, more easily consumed sounds of white pop music. And, as it can be reasonably argued that much Northern Soul is someone else's take on the Motown sound, it too falls into that area of being, for some, too poppy to really be Soul. Going down that route, however, potentially dismisses everything we would talk about here, but this does point up what still remains an area of controversy in Northern Soul: that there is often a very thin line (if anything) separating it from other types of music, and where the dividing line lies is the object of endless rows and much personal preference rolled out as material fact.

The Newbeats were a white act, and if their 'Bread and Butter', which was played way back, was played at a Northern Soul club now, it would be met with dismay. 'Run Baby Run', however, was a monster Northern Soul track that would still be much appreciated now, if not by everybody (certainly not by Soul purists). But then, objectively, 'Bread and Butter' is not dissimilar to Donnie Elbert's 'Little Piece of Leather', which is genuinely 'black' music, raucously in tune with early conceptions of what was 'rhythm and Soul', and would be danced to enthusiastically at the (reborn) Twisted Wheel now, even if regarded as a bit passé and RnB-ish at some other Northern Soul clubs. 'Run Baby Run' has the added advantage of a deep, dirty bass riff, not dissimilar to that in the Four Tops' 'I Can't Help Myself', which enables it to get away with its more pop-ish aspects, whereas 'Bread and Butter' has the added disadvantage of what many would regard as novelty lyrics. These are slim margins of acceptability, operating around unspoken, sometimes disputed, but much of the time informally agreed standards.

There is, generally, a noticeable difference between black and white voices, which helps define the 'Soul' sound, but this is less noticeable when singers sing in falsetto, in harmony or are overlaid with a powerful instrumental backing, and when the music is so fast that a soulful delivery is not easy to achieve, as is the case in much Northern Soul. Frankie Valli and the Four Seasons make much use of falsetto and seem to have been accepted as a Northern Soul act with little quibble. Moreover, some white singers do a passable black voice. For many of us, the discovery that Dean Parrish was white came as quite a shock. Conversely, Paintbox were, 'apparently', black[11], but not American, and although their 'Get Ready for Love' was spun at The Moon back in 1970-71, it sounds too 'poppy' to be well regarded in the Northern Soul scene in general, even if it gets the occasional outing on the Facebook 'Northern Soul' page.

---

[11] The apparent blackness of Paintbox is dubious. Their single 'Get Ready for Love' came with a picture sleeve that featured five young black guys, but this may have been a ruse, and it is likely that the band was made up mostly of former members of the 60s white beat group The Easybeats. See Warburton, Nick. Vanda and Young post-Easybeats: Paintbox, Moondance and Tramp. Garagehangover [online] Available: http://www.garagehangover.com/vandaandyoung/ [Accessed 23 June 2016]

Other grey-area acts, above, include John Miles, who is now widely known as a white rock act, having had a monster chart hit with 'Music' in the mid-1970s. His 'Why Don't You Love Me', however, found its way into many Northern Soul record collections at the start of the 70s. It would be an unlikely inclusion on any contemporary Northern Soul DJ's playlist now, but whether this is because it does not sound soulful enough, because he is now known as a non-Soul act, or because there are lots of better records that could be spun instead is not clear. Wayne Fontana's 'Something Keeps Calling Me Back' could be seen as an even stranger anomaly. Wayne is a white Mancunian and this track is the b-side of one of his major pop hits: the very sugary 'Pamela Pamela'. 'Something Keeps Calling Me Back', however, kicks off at a really fast, exciting pace and arguably fits the Northern Soul idiom, and even if for many Northern Soul fans it is a no-no, for many others it remains a guilty pleasure.

Instrumentals are, in general, an anomalous area for Soul. How a voiceless track projects Soul is an interesting question. The Mar-Keys, who played the instrumental backing tracks on some of the most indisputably soulful records of the 1960s, were, with the odd change of personnel, mostly white throughout most of the band's existence. A couple of anomalies from the late 60s/early 70s appear above. 'Sultana' by Titanic and 'The Kid' by Andre Brasseur are both bits of Euro pop that were played in proto-Northern Soul clubs at the time. 'Sultana' would now clear a Northern Soul dance floor quicker than you could say 'Abba's Greatest Hits'. 'The Kid' is still a floor-packer at current The Twisted Wheel, because of its historical connection with the place, but it would not be acceptable at most other Northern Soul venues.

Ultimately, what is acceptable as a Northern Soul record is a strange and malleable thing, which shifts over time and continues to be a matter of personal/group/club/area/era preference, divided opinion, informal negotiation, blind/deaf prejudice and nostalgia. A lot of it is not 'Soul' at all, but then the scene never promised that, and most aficionados do not mind. As will be discussed below, 'Northern Soul' is a name that was applied to an existing scene from outside, and that scene never did play just pure and only 'Soul'.

Other myths surround the matter of when many of these records came out. I once had an argument with someone who insisted that 'Hey Girl Don't Bother Me' by the Tams was not a Northern Soul record or even a 1960s record because it was a hit in 1971. The belief that 'when I first heard it' equals 'when it first came out' is not uncommon. This track was first released in 1964 on the exquisitely old-fashioned-sounding HMV (His Master's Voice) label in the UK (it was on ABC Paramount in the US). Before its popularity in the North's clubs prompted its re-release in the early 70s, it was extremely rare and very much sought-after. Stories circulated about copies of it changing hands for £20 a time, which was then about a week's wages for a working man. Such rarity and the timing of its peak in popularity make it one of the records that defined what a Northern Soul record was, but few would now give it house room.

In the same vein, what is also scarcely understood now is how obscure Tamla Motown once was in the UK. The tracks that many would regard as Motown's greatest were recorded between roughly 1964 and 1967 and, as mentioned above, this was before Britain had a pop music radio station[12]. All there was, officially, was the BBC's 'Light Programme', which played some pop, but whose format and remit overall had scarcely changed since the 1940s. There were, however, pirate radio stations that made listening to something other than the approved output an enjoyably illicit experience, if you had the impulse to look for them; and there was the odd TV pop music programme; and there were the clubs. So there was some interest in Soul, and Motown did have some hits in that time, but what is instructive is the fact that a major UK Motown tour in 1967 bombed. It played to three-quarters-empty halls because the label was so little known and its artistes had so small a fan base. It is also worth bearing in mind that following a label was an unusual thing then. Most UK labels published a broad spread of artistes; the fact that someone might buy a Rolling Stones record did not mean that they would become a fan of Decca records in general, and buying a few Beatles singles would be unlikely to make someone determined to own everything ever released on Parlophone. Motown's real UK success story came from the late 1960s into the early 70s, when so many tracks were re-issued because of the interest taken in them in the clubs and because Radio One DJs, such as Tony Blackburn and Mike Raven, championed them. 'Put Yourself in My Place' by The Elgins, 'Tears of a Clown' by the Miracles and 'Just a Little Misunderstanding' by the Contours are just a few of the mid-60s recordings that reached a broader UK public on re-release at the beginning of the 1970s. In his sleeve notes on the 1969 compilation album 'British Motown Chartbusters Volume 3', DJ Alan Freeman refers to 're-issue mania'. Seven of the sixteen tracks on the album were first released between 1964 and 1967. The Four Tops' 'I Can't Help Myself' reached number 23 in the UK charts when it was first released in 1965, but it got as far as number 10 in early 1970, after being re-released. On that second release, it became one of the key tracks that introduced my generation to American black music and made Tamla Motown a part of life.

The upshot of this is that that beaten-up old Tamla Motown 45 you have,

---

[12] Indeed, Motown did not have a UK label until 1965, when Tamla Motown came into existence. Up to that point, the records Motown chose to release in the UK came out on Stateside, Fontana, Oriole and London.

showing a date of, say, 1965, might well, if the TMG number is in the upper 600s or into the 700s, be the late-60s/early-70s re-release. The Four Tops' 'I Can't Help Myself', for example, was TMG 515 on its original release in 1965; the 1970 re-release has the number TMG 732.

There are, however, anomalies: Earl van Dyke's '6 by 6', for example, was a mid-60s recording, but if you pick up a UK copy, you will see that it has a release date of 1970 and the number TMG 759, which corresponds to Tamla Motown's releases of that date. This is because it was never released in the UK prior to that date. Of course, it was played and well known in UK clubs before then, but the copies that circulated were all imports (on the US 'Soul' record label – a Motown subsidiary). To add to the confusion, however, the B-side of that 1970 issue of '6 by 6' is 'All for You'. It is still TMG 759, of course, but its release date is shown as 1965. This is because 'All for You' was first released in 1965 as TMG 506. Are you still with me?

It was not only Motown's mid-60s output that was being re-released and making the charts at this time; tracks from other labels that had first gained popularity in the North's clubs were re-released and some became monster hits. 'I'm Gonna Run Away from You' by Tammi Lynn, 'At the Top of the Stairs' by the Formations and 'I Get the Sweetest Feeling' by Jackie Wilson are examples of records which have become so ubiquitous that it is hard now to imagine that they were once rare and known only to Northern Soul cognoscenti, but they were.

There are a few of what I would describe as 'turning point' records in the above in the 1969-71 period we are looking at here. 'Hey Girl Don't Bother Me' is one, being the first record that, for many of us, made visible concepts of rarity and high value amongst records. If it was a turning-point record, one of even greater significance was Leon Haywood's 'Baby Reconsider'. It was even rarer and more valuable. It had never been released in the UK; what few copies there of it were, were US imports; and its asking price – well over a working man's weekly wages – was completely out of reach for most of us, even if we knew where there was a copy to be bought. It was also a storming, fast, dynamic record; very different in that respect from the Tams' offering. In having these characteristics of rarity, a fast beat, the right style of sound and only existing as an import, it was, arguably, one of the first records to define what a Northern Soul record was, as the scene gelled into what it would become from this point onwards. The term 'Northern Soul' was still a long way from visibility at this point, but through records like 'Baby Reconsider', the expression 'Rare Soul' for the style of music on offer at these clubs now gained currency.

Another turning point record, for different reasons, was 'Spirit in the Sky' by Norman Greenbaum. Like many, I heard it at The Moon and bought it in 1970. In spite of it having girlie backing singers, layered vocals and a good earthy bass line beat for dancing to, there was something wrong about it. Although it shared those characteristics with Soul tracks, there were differences between it and the music I felt more strongly drawn to. It became apparent to my naive ears, and to those of others coming to terms with the same things, that there was something at stake here. It was not a Soul record. We understand distinguishing characteristics through what a thing is not like, as well as what it is like, and the difference between records like this and the likes of 'Baby Reconsider' started to define what was and was not the 'right' sort of music.

But back to my 'career' as a Northern Soul fanatic, which I did say I would outline for sceptics out there. I left school in summer 1971 and started work at what was then The North Western Gas Board as a Gas Engineering Technician Apprentice. The pay, being apprentice rates, wasn't great – eight quid a week to start with – but it was some money, and after I'd given my mum three quid keep, there was still a fiver to have some fun with. This wasn't a useless amount of money in an era when a pint of bitter was 11p, the going rate for getting into a night club was about 50p and a record that might be sold on Ebay now for a three-figure sum could be bought, all pristine and new, in the local record shop for 37½ p.

One of the well-known features of Northern Soul is that it traditionally involved travelling great distances to get to the best clubs. Up to this point I had only been able to get to local clubs – those in what became the Tameside area of Greater Manchester – but now, with my weekly fiver, I could go more or less anywhere. My first 'away trip' was Blackpool Mecca in the spring of 1972. This was closely followed by The Torch in Stoke-on-Trent – my first all-nighter – and I loved it. It was like that first moment in The Moon over again, but this time with even greater intensity. I suspect that your first all-nighter is like your first love: others may come and go, but nothing is quite like your first.

Then came those many other places that have gone down in Northern Soul folklore, and a few that may have been forgotten: The Pendulum, Caroline's and The Piccadilly Club in Manchester. There were also Rowntree's Sounds and Spring Gardens in Manchester, but these took the form more of 'disco pubs' than night clubs. There was Sale Mecca, a.k.a. 'The Blue Room'; a magnificent place, which had Ian Levine and Colin Curtis as regulars and therefore an amazing playlist, but which is often forgotten because it was a week-night event and many never experienced it. Then there were Druffies

*The Twisted Wheel, Whitworth Street, Manchester, in 2012. Pete Roberts, DJ and Promoter, stood outside. The Wheel was originally founded in Brazennose Street, Manchester in 1963, but soon moved to Whitworth Street, where it became one of the seminal Northern Soul clubs. It closed in 1971, but reopened in 2000. The Whitworth Street premise was demolished in 2013, but the Wheel lives on, a few hundred yards away on Princess Street. Photo credit: Stephen Riley. Permission obtained from the Twisted Wheel/Pete Roberts.*

in Dukinfield (Dukinfield Rugby Club); Wigan Casino; Talk of the North (Cleethorpes Pier and Winter Gardens); Queens Hall, Leeds; Cats Whiskers, Oldham; Tiffanies, Newcastle-under-Lyme; the St. Ives All-nighter; The Carousel, Manchester; Ritz All-Dayer, Manchester.

I drifted away from the scene in the late 70s. Like many of my peer group, I had reached an age where grown-up things like getting married, developing a career and buying a house had taken over, plus, still doing at 24 what you were doing at 14 seemed a bit off. The last all-nighter I went to was at The Carousel in Manchester in the late 70s. For the first time I felt completely out of place. The venue seemed to be packed with kids the age I had been when I first stumbled, blinking, into the darkness of The Moon, still wearing clothes I had discarded by the mid-70s. I had more in common with the bouncers. It was time to move on. It's strange to think that what I felt too old for at 24 feels eminently reasonable nearly four decades on.

I came back to the scene first in the mid-1990s, attending the Kings Hall, Blackburn all-nighters once or twice and, later, the Blackpool Tower Weekender, plus the odd trip to Hyde United's social club in Greater Manchester, and a few events in pub function rooms in Glossop. Then, on moving south, I became a regular at Cagneys, The Belvedere, The Railway Club, the Student Union and 'Soul on the Sea', all in Bournemouth. I also went a few times to Bishopstoke Memorial Hall, and once each (so far) to Farnborough Soul Club, North Petherton Rugby Club (Bridgwater), the Totton All-Dayer in Southampton, London's 100 Club and an event in a hotel in Exeter, the name of which now escapes me. I have also made many visits to the revived Twisted Wheel, at Whitworth Street, then at Alter Ego on Princess Street in Manchester, and quite a few to a burgeoning event called Glastonbury Soul, which takes place at the town's football club. I have also been to various pub function-room events, of variable quality, in Greater Manchester and Somerset.

# Just what is this Northern Soul 'genre' of music?

Arguments occur over and again about what should be called a 'Northern Soul' record. Some want to dismiss some things because they are not Soul records at all, even though they were very popular on the scene. They might even do this whilst, themselves, still liking other non-Soul records that were played. The degree of soulfulness might be given as the deciding factor, but this tends to be subjective. For example, both Frankie Valli and the Four Seasons and Gary Lewis and the Playboys are white acts whose music was played on the Northern Soul scene, but, whilst the former are likely to be considered by many as an acceptable group, the latter would be dismissed by most as a pop act and an example of things going awry on the scene.

These anomalies produce frequent arguments in which the goal is to define Northern Soul as a 'genre', so that it can be clear what should and should not be considered acceptable. I would argue, however, that this is probably an impossible task.

We might, quite reasonably, say that there is no such musical genre as Northern Soul. Certainly, what we can say is that (unless we count latter-day copyists) none of the musicians who made the music of the heyday of Northern Soul had ever even heard of Northern Soul when they made their Northern Soul records. Many were subsequently surprised to hear that they had made a Northern Soul record, and many others have gone to their graves having recorded a Northern Soul classic without having ever having heard of Northern Soul.

Let us just deal with the obvious bit first, for the benefit of any newcomers or non-Brits reading this: what Northern Soul does not refer to is Soul music made in the northern US states, as opposed to that made in southern US states. Many recordings made by Stax records, for example, based in the southern city of Memphis, are an important part of Northern Soul, as are many cut at Muscle Shoals in Alabama. Northern Soul, as we have come to understand it, is or was a music scene in the UK, which reputedly emerged in the North of England, hence the name. For most Northern Soul fans, where in the US a record was recorded (and in some cases whether it was recorded in the US at all) was and remains a non-issue.

More on that will follow, but now back to the question of 'genre'. A dictionary definition of the word is as follows:

genre[13]      [zhahn-ruh; French zhahn-ruh]

Examples
- Word Origin
- noun, plural genres

[zhahn-ruh z; French zhahn-ruh]

1. a class or category of artistic endeavor having a particular form, content, technique, or the like:
    the genre of epic poetry; the genre of symphonic music.

2. Fine Arts.
    i. paintings in which scenes of everyday life form the subject matter.
    ii. a realistic style of painting using such subject matter.

3. genus; kind; sort; style. adjective

4. Fine Arts. of or pertaining to genre.

5. of or pertaining to a distinctive literary type.

The bit that counts here is 'a class or category of artistic endeavor (sic) having a particular form'. The problem of defining Northern Soul as a genre is that the music is of more than just one kind; it does not all correspond to one 'particular form'. Also, as mentioned above, the artists who made the music had no inkling of the concept 'Northern Soul' when they made it and therefore could not have consciously made 'Northern Soul Music'. Northern Soul has the rare distinction of being defined not by the circumstances of its production, but of those of its consumption, and not at the time it was made, but afterwards. But then, maybe it comes down to a matter of semantics: just what do we mean by 'class' and 'category' and by 'particular form'? These could all be quite leaky terms.

[13] Dictionary.com [online] Available: http://www.dictionary.com/browse/genre [Accessed 23 November 2014]

Northern Soul is dance music, so it has to have a beat to dance to. However, most pop music has a beat you can dance to, whilst very little of it would be called Northern Soul, so the beat alone does not help us. Some would think of Northern Soul as all being recorded by black Americans in the 1960s, but much of it is not by black singers and much comes from later, and sounds like it does. Also, much of it is not necessarily very 'soulful', if we define that through likenesses to records such as Otis Redding's 'I've Been Loving You Too Long', which is powerfully pleading and gives a sense of being sung 'from the soul'. But then, maybe, it is the overall 'style' of the music that makes it some kind of Soul music, even if it lacks the depth of a more profound Soul record. 'Soul' might be hard to define, but we know a record that has the right 'sound', because we have listened to so many others like it. This might get us closer, but even this is a weak theory because there is so much variation within what has been drawn into Northern Soul. Within the Northern Soul canon there are tracks by crooner, Mel Torme; rockers, Little Richard and Mitch Ryder; country-and-western singers, Charlie Rich and Ronnie Milsap; folk singer, Nancy Ames; one-time teeny-bop idol, Paul Anka; English DJ, Tony Blackburn; American DJ, Frankie Crocker; Elvis Presley (do I need to provide a definition for him?); swamp rocker, Tony Joe White; cabaret singer, Solomon King; Soul-jazz-funksters, Earth, Wind and Fire and The Commodores (before they turned into balladeers); Spanish rock outfit, Los Canarios; The Baltimore and Ohio Marching Band – a marching band from Baltimore and Ohio; Belgian Keyboard player, Andre Brasseur; trouser-splitting enigma, P J Proby; gospel singer, Clara Ward; jazz legends, The Crusaders and Nancy Wilson; former doo-wop-ists, The Drifters; the probably indefinable, Gil Scott-Heron; funk rockers, Black Nasty; Irish pop singer, Muriel Day; American comedian, Bill Cosby; various English pop singers, including Lorraine Silver, Helen Shapiro and Waynes Gibson and Fontana; as well as assorted TV and film themes, such as 'Hawaii Five-O', 'Rat Race' and the theme from the children's puppet show 'Joe 90'; plus some 1970s 'disco' tracks; and more...

I can imagine many reading the above will feel their toes curling as they do so and, in fairness, what some of these instances really represent is a moment when a singer has moved out of their usual comfort zone to have a crack at the Soul idiom, rather than Northern Soul DJs occasionally succumbing to the appeal of folk music, country-and-western or film soundtracks. But that is not always so, and in some instances it is the case that Northern Soul has extended its remit to include the unlikely and the not-terribly-good. Whatever the case, like it or not, all of these artists and tracks were played in some places at some times under the banner of 'Northern Soul', and this list indicates the breadth of styles of music played and the difficulty of calling all of this one 'genre' of music or one 'particular form'. Some deal with these dodgy anomalous tracks by saying that they were played by lousy DJs, and the music does not represent 'real' Northern Soul, but since 'Northern Soul' has no reliable definition other than 'it was played at Northern Soul clubs', this is not a watertight way of thinking either. Moreover, some of the records that many would want to dismiss in this way are still loved by some. A recent argument on Facebook produced people who said they loved Wigan's Ovation's insipid cover version of The Invitations' classic 'Skiing in the Snow' and preferred it to the original. Some of these individuals did not know until that point that the Invitations' original existed and, on hearing it for the first time, found it a bit wanting; their ears having been tuned to the cover version for a lifetime. And even the 'Theme from Joe 90' still has some fans.

Maybe the best way to categorise Northern Soul is as a club scene that encompassed a wide range of music with, at its centre, a danceable, 4-4 beat, Motown-esque sound and black voices, but leant more towards pop than to earlier traditions of Blues, Gospel and Rhythm-and-Blues. However, pulls from that centre went in all directions, and some tendencies pulled so far that they reached breaking point. Thus, the descriptor of the music follows the name of the scene, so 'Northern Soul' is defined as the music played at Northern Soul clubs, whatever it sounds like if played in another context. The Northern Soul scene could also be (and was) called a 'disco' or 'discotheque' scene, but the word 'club' has become more prominent since, to distinguish it from the mid/late-70s general 'disco' scene, which brought the term 'disco' into disrepute. I will say more on this in a separate section below.

It needs also to be borne in mind that the term 'Northern Soul' came late to the scene. Though first coined by Dave Godin in the late 60s[14], for most of Northern Soul's heyday, the term was unknown; therefore there was no compulsion to play what fitted whatever definition it might be perceived to have. I think I first heard the term in 1974; others think they may have heard it in 1973. In fairness, however, the terms 'Soul' and 'Rare Soul' were bandied about before that, so there was the expectation that black American music was at the core; the degree of slippage into other things remaining contentious. The club that many would regard as the one in which the body of music that came to be called Northern Soul was given its shape was The Twisted Wheel in Manchester. Although it played predominantly black American music, it did not confine itself to Soul, to the fastest available beat

---

[14] Famously, Dave Godin 'invented' the term Northern Soul by accident, but precisely when is not clear. He had spotted that the northern football fans who invaded his London record shop every Saturday, when their team was in town to play Chelsea, Arsenal etc., were seeking a particular style of sound, different from the slower, deeper and funkier sounds favoured by his London-based customers. Identifying the trend, he selected from his stock and placed into separate boxes types of sounds they would be seeking: Soul that northern clubbers liked; Soul for northerners; Northern Soul. The term didn't go public until Blues and Soul magazine published a Dave Godin article on The Twisted Wheel in 1970; even then, it did not make its way immediately into common use.

or only to black American acts. Coming out of the Mod scene, it was a place where the appreciation of American black music was central, but that was not the only thing played. White RnB acts like Georgie Fame, Spencer Davis and Zoot Money were also enthusiastically received. However, artistes like these became sidelined as the scene began to define itself and as the concept of 'Rare Soul' emerged at the end of the 1960s/beginning of the 1970s.

If the 'Soul' bit in 'Northern Soul' is dubious, then so is the 'Northern' bit. As we have seen above and from the associated footnote, Dave Godin created the term accidentally. It was just a casual term – a convenient way of organising part of his London record shop. It was never intended to define a musical style or club scene. If The Twisted Wheel came to be the defining Northern Soul club, that is only because it kept on doing what it was doing long enough for things to mutate and get noticed there. In its early guise, the Wheel was one of many similar clubs in towns and cities across the country playing RnB and 'Rhythm and Soul', including London, which had got an early start on this due to the Mod scene emerging there first. Even as 'Northern Soul' clubs extricated themselves from that history, punters and clubs were not just in the North. Clubs like The Catacombs in Wolverhampton, Chateau Impney in Droitwich, The Lantern in Market Harborough and Up the Junction in Crewe were significant, and many of the movers and shakers who formed the scene were from the Midlands. It's not hard to imagine that a bunch of football fans from Nottingham or Stoke, piling into Dave Godin's shop on a Saturday afternoon, would have sounded sufficiently northern to a Londoner's ears to be bundled in with the Mancunians and Scousers and labelled with the same epithet. And maybe the cliché that, from a London perspective, everything north of Watford Gap is 'North' comes into play. But, whatever the case, since it was at first such a casual term, it was never going to be modified to take account of all the variables – 'Northern, Scottish and Midlands Soul' just doesn't have the same ring.

What I believe we are ultimately looking at here is a change in the meaning of the term 'Northern Soul', between the time when Dave Godin first used it, to when it came into general use: I believe that Dave Godin, when using the term in the first instance, meant the style of soul music preferred by the clubs of the North, and that changed to meaning a specific kind of music called 'Northern Soul', even though there was no such genre or music of that name, and this has left people floundering ever since in trying to define what is not really definable.

We can see a parallel in 'Impressionism' – the term applied to a 'movement' in art in the late nineteenth and early twentieth centuries. The term was applied by a critic, looking at what the artists had done; it was not chosen by the artists themselves, and they developed their work without any knowledge that this would someday be lumbered with the label 'Impressionism'. The result is that artists like Manet and Monet are lumped together, as if working to a common set of ideas when, in spite of their almost identical names, their work has little in common. Similarly, the term 'Northern Soul' was applied to the scene from the outside and was generally not welcomed by those within it, who went from 'Soul' or 'Rare Soul' fans to 'Northern Soul' fans, at someone else's behest, and went on to have their dancing styles, attitudes towards drugs, and fashion preferences distorted by media commentators, and new arrivals on the scene who had bought into the myths, and by stereotyping.

As the term 'Northern Soul' became visible, everyone I knew on the scene was annoyed by it. Northerners felt patronised, Midlanders felt marginalised. Personally, like many, I only use it with reluctance, because it has come to have a meaning that most people understand to a degree: it's a kind of clumsy shorthand. When I am among friends who were around at the time, we are more likely to call it just the 'Soul scene', as we did way back then.

The result of the widespread application of this term is, I would argue, destructive. Once a thing has a name, people start to create definitions, rules, histories, inclusions, exclusions, and more. I will argue below that this has contributed in no small way to the scene's ossification and museumification.

## What is the appeal of Northern Soul?

We can look at this in three ways: the objective appeal of the music, the appeal of the music in the context of what else was available, and the appeal of the scene as a cultural phenomenon. We might also consider what the appeal is to new generations getting into Northern Soul.

There is a problem in describing the appeal of the music when, as seen above, it varies so much, but if we look at the core sound, then maybe we can get somewhere. So, (generally), there would be a Motown-esque feel; a sometimes fast, always danceable, beat; passionate lyrics, passionately delivered; and powerful, often orchestrated, backing music. It can be argued that the real appeal of the music is that it has the best of all worlds: the power, pace and pounding beat of Rock; the heart-wrenching pain of Blues; the soaring passion of Gospel; and some of the musical breadth and intensity of Classical orchestral music. Add to all that, dancing passionately, fluently and without inhibition in an atmospheric nightclub, and the sensation becomes irresistible. Add to it, further, the odd bit of uplifting medication, and the effect is transcendental, celestial, ecstatic. The thrill is beyond words and can only be understood by doing it. It is easy to see why Northern Soul aficionados are so devoted to, and speak so passionately about, their music.

I recall a critic, Dave Godin, probably, likening the Northern Soul single to the operatic aria. At this distance, I am unable to find the reference, but the point – whether he made it or not – stands some scrutiny: the aria is a discrete song within an opera, it usually tells an emotive tale, has a memorable melody, and is quite short; it was the powerful, passionate, emotive 'single', before the single was invented. If the emotive and aural effects are not dissimilar to the Northern Soul record, Northern Soul has the added benefit that you can dance to it. This becomes especially apparent in songs like Tobi Legend's 'Time Will Pass You By', which, in the universality of its lyrics, as well as its style and passionate delivery, could be an aria, or at least a show song, whilst its pace makes it an irresistible dance track.

In addition to the thrill of the sound and experience overall, many tracks have electrifying intros which are hard to resist and pull you in. There are exceptions, but it is fair to say that many Northern Soul records are not by pop groups, in the traditional sense of 4 or 5 geezers with guitars and a drum kit. Rather, they are collaborations between writers, Soul singers, producers and highly experienced studio musicians, who deeply understand their craft and how to generate a feeling. The effect is music which is accomplished in so many ways and knows how to get into your psyche. This is a handful of tracks that have powerfully engaging intros, and I would suggest that anyone who is new to Northern Soul and would like to get into it goes to some of these first:

I Can't Get Enough – Johnny Sayles
You're Gonna Make Me Love You – Sandi Sheldon
Prove Yourself a Lady – James Bounty
Breakout – Mitch Ryder and the Detroit Wheels
Devil with a Blue Dress On/Good Golly Miss Molly – Mitch Ryder and the Detroit Wheels
I'm Gonna Love You a Long Long Time – Patti and the Emblems
World Without Sunshine – Sandra Phillips
One Wonderful Moment – The Shakers
Soul Time – Shirley Ellis
I Got to Find Me Somebody – The Vel-Vets

Another appeal of the scene was its socio-political associations. The emergence of the Northern Soul scene coincides with the rise of the American Black Civil Rights movement in the USA, which was frequently in the UK news at the time, as were the assassinations of Bobby Kennedy, Martin Luther King and others who stood up for the rights of black Americans. No-one with a soul could fail to be moved by what was happening or to be supportive of such a palpably just cause, but, for working-class kids, the association was perhaps a little closer to home.

No-one could seriously suggest that working-class British northerners experienced the discrimination and abuse that black Americans did in that period, but that does not equate by any means to saying that class disadvantage was not an issue – it was. Ours was a class-riven society, then. Northern Soul emerged in the same decade as the Lady Chatterley obscenity trial; the one in which the prosecutor asked 'Is it a book you would even wish your wife or servants to read?' That paternalistic attitude, the view that workers and wives were beneath a level at which they could be trusted to think for themselves, was just one moment when the class system, with its automatic view that the lower orders needed the control of their betters, reared its ugly head. More often, the class system did its business more silently. Only now are we hearing that working-class children, abused by high-ranking establishment paedophiles in the 1970s and 80s, had their evidence dismissed because they were 'unreliable witnesses'; 'unreliable witness' evidently being code for 'working-class witness who is not especially articulate or confident in the world of educated legal professionals', or possibly even 'working-class witness who is a threat to someone in a prominent position'. We have also heard from some abuse survivors that the paedophiles themselves told the kids they abused that they, the victims, could not protest because the abuser's word would be given primacy because of their social position; that effectively wealthy, prominent or upper-class abusers were above the law. In the class-dominated thinking of the time, in any dispute between a working-class person and a middle- or upper-class one, the working-class type would be deemed a liar because it was inconceivable that an upper-class person would do anything wrong; and even if s/he did, it was just a foible, an uncomfortable but forgivable peccadillo, and 'one had to look after one's own'. In the logic of the time, it was more important to protect wealthy and powerful people than to have justice done. In the words of the BBC's news online magazine: 'pre-Savile, when a person came forward with an allegation of abuse, their [the police's] knee-jerk response was often to set about undermining his or her credibility'.[15]

Those kinds of high-handed attitudes fed through to daily life in various ways: the snobbish ways in which you would be treated by middle-class people, the way people like you would be portrayed in the media, the sense of disempowerment you would feel in dealing with authority, and the negative presuppositions you would face before the Law, not to mention the kicking you would get from the police as part of your encounter with the Law. All of this fed into a strong feeling of solidarity with black Americans and enhanced the connection felt to their music, some of which made direct references to the Civil Rights cause. Also significant is that fact that Tamla Motown actually published three of Dr Martin Luther King's speeches, making concrete the link between this music and Civil Rights. It is not surprising, then, that Northern Soul adopted as its unofficial logo the black fist salute made famous by John Carlos and Tommie Smith at the 1968 Olympics, and that late-60s Northern Soul fans started wearing one black glove as part of their regalia.

For those of us who came to Northern Soul at the end of the sixties/beginning of the seventies, the competition was easy to resist. The alternatives ran from Prog Rock to Glam Rock: the pretentious to the preposterous – from a

---

[15] Thomas, Ceri. 6 October 2015. What's the truth about the VIP 'paedophile ring'? BBC News Online Magazine [online] Available http://www.bbc.co.uk/news/magazine-34442292 [Accessed 20 September 2017]

Soul boy's perspective. Po-faced lads with long hair, bad skin, wire-rimmed glasses and ex-army trench coats would plague the youth club Dansette with Spooky Tooth, Yes and King Crimson LPs. On the telly, sequinned drag acts sang nursery-rhyme lyrics like 'poppa rumbo rumbo hey poppa Joe coconut' and 'metal guru, is it you?', and a Baco Foil-clad kiddie-twiddler wanted to know if we wanted to be in his gang. The answer was an emphatic NO! Hard-arsed skinhead clothes and attitudes, the credible music of an oppressed people and the throbbing heart of a dark, smoky Soul club were the only way to go. The competition really was nothing.

It seems ironic now, but back in those days, we Soul boys, with our leatherette boxes of Stax, Motown and Reggae records, were looked down upon by the Prog Rock brigade. Theirs was intelligent music: all mystical, esoteric lyrics, 20-minute guitar solos and the vague promise of some kind of revelation – the meaning of life, probably. In contrast, ours was – so we were told – a mishmash of mindless, repetitive, 7-inch, pop-tune love-ditties. Not only does that miss the point, it is an arbitrary distinction anyway. Prog Rock's lyrics do not contain any profound wisdom and the progressiveness of the sound is dubious. Indeed, many Prog Rock songs are also simple love songs, even if some of them are placed in the imaginary world of Guinevere and Sir Lancelot.

Bob Dylan was also a name posited by the long-haired listeners to this 'more intellectual' music, and in his case the claim of something worthwhile was more valid. Those were good tunes and good songs, if you could get past the nasal whining. Yet, this still misses the point. Different kinds of music appeal in different ways. Bob Dylan's music could not deliver the thrill that a fast-paced, passionately-sung Soul song did, nor could it give you the cool, darkly exciting scene that went with it.

The patronising and paternalistic attitudes of the followers of those kinds of music were indicative of its status as 'older brother's' music, and of the path it proffered, via the student dorm to the bourgeois dinner party or the late-night spliff, to an esoteric truth that never really existed. Northern Soul, on the other hand, inhabited an anarchic, dangerous, working-class world of boot boys, skinhead girls and chemist-shop burglars. It was not led by record companies, nor did it come with seductive psychedelic record sleeves or the promise of some profound but never quite properly delivered wisdom. Northern Soul was bottom-up: the people on the scene were its driving force and its consumers. The music already existed, but it was obscure and did not give up its treasure easily. It had to be unearthed by the untrained, who were learning as they went along. Much of it only existed in dusty warehouses, thousands of miles away. To add to the problem, Northern Soul could not be searched for on the basis of 'I know what it is – I just don't know where it is': each black 7-inch disc could contain something wonderful or something awful; there was no way of knowing without finding it and playing it. This applied even if the artiste had already made an impact on the Northern Soul scene, because no artiste made solely Northern Soul music. You might stumble on a promising looking Gene Chandler track, only to discover that it was a ballad. The rareness of the records mattered too; it offered the thrill of being an insider in possession of precious objects and knowledge.

Northern Soul did not promise the meaning of life, it gave life meaning. You went from being a scruffy working-class nobody to someone who took great care in the choice and cut of his/her clothes, an authority on rare, exotic artefacts, and an expert dancer with techniques and moves all your own, and you became part of an underground scene seductively incomprehensible to those outside of it. Dobie Gray's 'The 'In' Crowd' seemed absolutely made for us (even if it had seemed absolutely made for the Mod scene a few years earlier).

An appeal of Northern Soul which is not much talked about concerns the relationship between, particularly, the male revellers and what they were able to extract from the scene that they would never have otherwise experienced. In working-class Britain in that era, expressions of male emotion, or the concept of a male having (let alone showing) a feminine side, were social suicide. Dancing was a clumsy, begrudgingly-engaged-with thing, to be tolerated only as a means of chatting-up a girl. Men were men, and these were not manly traits. Going to a Northern Soul club was to experience a freedom of emotion and movement that was not otherwise available to working-class youth. Basking in the beauty of the music, immersing oneself into the passion of the lyrics and doing whatever felt right on the dancefloor were liberating experiences, which were transformative and not imaginable elsewhere in working-class life. On the dancefloor of a Northern Soul club, a working-class kid could experience the pleasure other classes get from poetry, orchestral music and dance. This is not to suggest that a Smokey Robinson lyric equates to a T.S Eliot poem, or that a two minute vinyl wonder is the equal of a Beethoven symphony, but I would argue that there is a kind of equivalence. Indeed, the spiritual engagement might well be more profound, because the experience of Northern Soul in an all-nighter is enhanced by the exquisite synthesis of sound, words and movement, creating a transcendent whole. There is also something in the fact that the dancing is public. There are overtones of the '*Billy Elliot*'[16] story in this. A working-class male at that time would have been ridiculed and had his sexuality challenged for taking an interest in dance, but on the Northern Soul dancefloor there was nothing to hide and nothing to

---
[16] Billy Elliot. (2000) Film. Dir. Stephen Daldry

justify. On the contrary, the dancer could be proud of what he did: the energy, skill and inventiveness were not only enjoyed as physical expression, they were emphatically visible. This became enshrined by the invention of Northern Soul dancing competitions. This brings us to another Northern Soul myth: that everyone did those eye-catching front-drops, backdrops and spins.

Although the cliché of the leaping, diving Northern-Soul dancer is the one most well-known to a lay public, most dancers kept on their feet and just danced. This was and remains fast, energetic and inventive dancing, which might contain more creativity than the more visually striking leaps and backdrops, but it is overshadowed in the media by those more dramatic moves. Those dancefloor callisthenics were relatively rare before the media came to Northern Soul and focused on that aspect in their coverage because of its spectacularity. Apart from any other consideration, on a crammed dancefloor there is little room for leaping about, and those who did so in those circumstances could be a flailing menace. It is also questionable whether a person can be in that state of rapturous engagement with the music, described above, when they are girding their loins for their next Triple Salchow. But, also, such moves were considered by many as uncool, because they were informed by the media's appropriation and reinvention of Northern Soul, and because they were outside of the 'cool' impulse that guided the original Mod ethos that was the precursor of the scene. I will say more on this in a separate section, below.

There are others better placed to know what the appeal of Northern Soul is to young people, now, but interviews indicate that it is much the same as it was to those who loved the music first time around. The acceptability of such old music – perhaps equivalent to my generation becoming fanatical about Glenn Miller – is an aspect of a broader cultural shift, in which, instead of each new fashion rapidly following on the heels of the last one, many things co-exist. For a young person to follow old musical styles is no longer social suicide; all forms are there to be chosen from, as you please. It might also be argued that this music, made in real, echoey 1960s studios, with the real thrub of bass guitars, booms on bass drums, cracks on snares and crashes of cymbals, as opposed to computer-managed perfection, has something more powerful and imperfectly human about it. Catch this sound on vinyl, too, with its deep crunchy grooves, in place of the shrill tinge of digital sound, and the impact can be even more thrilling.

## When was Northern Soul?

This is going to be a controversial area, but I will stick my head above the parapet, make an argument and justify it. Research has not revealed precisely when in the late-60s Dave Godin stuck that fateful sign on that particular box in his record shop. I have seen 1968 posted online, but I am not sure how that could be reliably known. In any case, to an extent, that need not matter, because the term did not gain currency until much later. What that gives us to focus on, then, is the question of when Northern Soul, without its name, gelled into having the characteristics that made it what it was and when it lost them and moved on into being something else.

I would argue that, even though The Twisted Wheel, The Catacombs and other clubs had for some years been playing the records and filling the Northern Soul club role, the turning point came toward the end of the 1960s, and the scene had mutated properly into Northern Soul scene as we came to know it by the start of the 1970s. I say this for particular reasons.

Skinheads refer to the 'Spirit of 69' – the moment when that sub-cult enjoyed its heyday. Skinhead clothes, attitudes and music – Reggae, Ska, Bluebeat – were, at that point, closely intertwined with Soul, and many of us who got into Soul got into those West Indian musical styles too. For many of us Soul fans, however, the violence of skinheadry was something we did not want, and the racism, including 'Paki bashing' (which no-one seems to want to remember now), was both unacceptable and embarrassingly incongruous in a music scene that centred on black music. Reggae had the additional disadvantage of having gone over ground, to the extent that it was visible in pop charts and was the object of purpose-made records like 'Skinhead Moon Stomp'[17]. Also, it did not provide the rapid Soul beat that had become the preferred sound. As 'Rare Soul', the prototype of Northern Soul, defined itself, Reggae and other West Indian music were jettisoned, along with many of the excesses of skinhead behaviour. The slower and rawer American RnB sounds that had

---

[17] Symarip, 1969.

been popular in the mid-60s had also been declining in popularity for some time, as had most of the white RnB acts that had been acceptable in the Mod era. The pressure from amphetamine-fuelled revellers for the up-tempo beat had been changing the sound as early as 1967. In an interview given in 1985, Roger Eagle, early DJ at The Twisted Wheel and the man regarded by many as one of the godfathers of the scene that came before Northern Soul, said the following: "...after 4 years at the Wheel it was down to that one fast Northern Soul dance beat which became very boring and that's why I left in mid '67"[18]. Whereas these various musical styles had co-existed for some time, and the part of it that would become Northern Soul had been visible enough to irritate Roger Eagle as far back as 1967, the completion of the exclusion of the other styles reached its conclusion at the end of the 1960s and the genesis of Northern Soul was complete. As if to rubber-stamp this, Dave Godin went to The Twisted Wheel in Manchester in 1970 and wrote a highly influential article for Blues and Soul magazine, based on the visit, which definitively marked out the Soul scene in the North as a distinct entity.

The following tract from Hinkley Soul Club, on the Twisted Wheel, is indicative:

*Roger Eagle continued to DJ at the club, mixing Muddy Waters with James Brown, The Drifters and Chuck Berry. It was only when the more elusive UK releases of American origin were started to be played that the Wheel came into a class of it's (sic) own. One thing that made the Twisted Wheel different was that the club had a record collection of it's (sic) own, locked up securely behind those bike wheels... It is unclear as to whether the sounds being played back in 1965-1967 belonged to Roger Eagle or the Wheel itself, but just look at these examples... "Open The Door To Your Heart" - Darrell Banks, "That's What I Wanna Know" - James Carr, "Candy" - The Astors, "Walking Up A One Way Street" - Willie Tee. Was this the real beginning of Northern Soul?*

*Roger Eagle moved away from the Wheel in 1967, but continued to DJ at the Blue Note club, later opening his own club, Stax. The DJ rosta was soon augmented by the arrival of an old Hinckley friend, Brian Rae. By now, the R&B bias had been largely replaced by a more Soul-oriented style, and the rarer the better. The real turning point in the Wheel's history came, however, at Christmas 1968, when the Wheel's record collection was stolen. The focus shifted immediately to the DJ's individual collections. In 1969, the arrival of American imports really solidified what is now the structure of Northern Soul. The others in the DJ team, namely Rob Bellars, Carl Dene, Phil Saxe, Paul Davis, Les Cockell and Brian "45" Phillips began playing more and more US music. Competition between the DJs was*

---

[18] The Twisted Wheel [online] Available: http://www.twistedwheel.com/page13.html [Accessed 8 December 2014]

> *fierce, and those with access to US importers soon rose to the top. Rob Bellars in particular often took a chance and ordered records "blind" from the States... one such record was by an unknown artist named Sandi Sheldon. Rob is also credited as being the first DJ to "cover up" a particularly interesting track to prevent anyone else from obtaining it.*
>
> *It was around 1969 that the Northern Soul style of dancing started to develop. The now standard side-to-side shuffling style was being enhanced by more adventurous acrobatic routines and spins. The undisputed star of the dance floor at the Wheel was Frank Booper. It is said that Frank had the ability to stop the dance floor entirely while people gathered round to watch.*[19]

This shows us that music we would now think of as 'Northern Soul' was played alongside other styles, way back when it was first recorded. It also describes the gradual marginalisation of those other styles, as Northern Soul (even without that name) rose to the top toward the end of the 60s. It further describes instances of acrobatic dancing, which was still a rarity back then and enough of a novelty that others stopped dancing to watch. (See separate section on acrobatic dancing.)

One of the key defining features of the Northern Soul scene was that it was bottom-up and anarchic. The fact that the music was made by others made the scene different from that other well-known anarchic milieu: Punk. However, the artistes who created Northern Soul were half a world away and had no knowledge of it, and the scene itself was created and defined by the people involved in it. It was not pushed along by advertisements, mainstream musical trends, what was going on in the media or record company promotions. Indeed, the scene thrived on what was not even known until it was found by those directly involved.

We can, therefore, set out these defining features for Northern Soul as a scene:

- it was based on danceable Soul, plus some white RnB that came close to Soul;
- it eschewed West Indian styles, like Reggae, and American styles which did not have the right beat, such as funk, slow Soul and early, raw RnB;
- it moved forward by playing-out records and debuting new ones – both new recordings and previously unheard old material;
- the rarity of the records mattered, which meant that new records had less kudos;
- it was anarchic and bottom-up: it was indifferent to mainstream music fads and it had no truck with influence and leadership from the media

---
[19] Hinkley Soul Club [online] http://rareSoul.org.uk/hinckleySoulclub/wheel.htm [Accessed 25 January 2017]

or record companies, even if punters on the scene were grateful, once the record companies had spotted the demand, to get their hands on re-releases of tracks long hungered-for but to that point unattainable.

1974 through to 1975 was the period in which Northern Soul went over ground. Major record companies were now involved, knew what material in their back catalogues was in demand and were re-releasing it. Record companies had spasmodically spotted club-derived interest in their back catalogues previously – in the late 60s – and re-released tracks: 'Earthquake' by Al 'TNT' Braggs, released in 1966 and again in 1968, for example. Starting in 1968, Dave Godin's Soul City label was clearly aimed a Soul cognoscenti audience and a good deal of its output was Northern Soul. There was a flurry of re-releases at the beginning of the 70s, featuring labels such as Mojo and Contempo. But what happened from 1974 onwards was something different and bigger. The scene had a name and was an identifiable entity that could be appealed to via marketing and the targeting of products.

By now, Pye's 'Disco Demand' series of single re-releases was under way. In 1974, they had released the compilation LP 'Disco Demand's Solid Soul Sensations: 16 Previously Unreleased Northern Soul Sounds', with sleeve notes by Ian Levine. Their 'Great Disco Demands' compilation LP, featuring Northern Soul tracks with a 'what-Wigan-Casino-plays' skew, was released in 1975, with sleeve notes by Wigan Casino's Russ Winstanley. A year later RCA issued the compilation 'Jumping at the Go Go: 20 Great Northern Soul Hits', with sleeve notes by Richard Searling and an embarrassing cover, featuring cartoons of a rosy-cheeked boy and girl wearing the Northern Soul stereotype look. These LPs were indicative of the fact that the phenomenon that was Northern Soul was by now fully understood at the corporate level and that there was a large, non-specialist market for the record companies to pursue. They were also indicative of the imminent exhaustion of the resource that Northern Soul relied upon: 'new' old records. These LPs, along with many single re-releases and DJs fiercely competing with each other to unearth everything that remained to be unearthed, pushed the scene rapidly to the point where much of what was there to be discovered had been discovered.

As the number of obscure Soul records waiting to be found moved inevitably toward exhaustion, diverse strategies were forming to fill the gap and cash in. Strange 'new' musical concoctions started to appear, made by taking the backing tracks from various well-known Soul songs, laying a bit of a bit of synthesiser over them, and pressing them as instrumental versions by invented bands; Ian Levine took the Northern Soul idiom and made new, purpose-built Northern Soul tracks; and, at Wigan Casino, Russ Winstanley and friends played anything from the 1960s with a backbeat, regardless of how poppy it sounded, and passed it off as 'Northern Soul'. Outsiders to the scene cottoned-on. Indian-born, England-based music producer, Biddu, came up with a track called 'Northern Dancer'. Leslie Charles, from Essex, under the stage name of Billy Ocean, had a hit with the Motown/Northern Soul clone record 'Love Really Hurts Without You'. The Top of the Pops stage was graced by Wigan's Ovation – who to this point, under another name, had been a working-men's club act – performing their cover version of the Invitations' 'Skiing in the Snow'. An advert for a toy was remixed with crowd chants from a football match and made the pop charts as 'Footsee' by Wigan's Chosen Few. And then the clichés and the cashing-in become wholly visible; a point clearly affirmed when The Goodies – a television trio regarded as humorous by some sectors of society – had a hit with the parody record 'Black Pudding Bertha (The Queen of Northern Soul)', which, though dreadful, was no more cringe-inducing a sight on Top of the Pops than Wigan's Ovation.

The publicity surrounding Wigan Casino had made it a magnet for those who wanted to be involved with the latest thing, which was now 'Northern Soul'. The place became crowded with new people who, the week before, had been listening to Alvin Stardust, Showaddywaddy and the Bay City Rollers, and had now rejected that in favour of donning the Northern Soul uniform of baggies and bowling shirt, and emulating the acrobatic dance styles that had been presented by the media as a necessary part of the scene. An individual whom I will not name, but will describe as a well-known West Midlands record collector, holder of blunt opinions, and owner of an encyclopaedic knowledge of (Northern) Soul, described the place as having become a 'circus' by 1975. Many of those who had seen Wigan Casino as a saviour of the scene in 1973, when The Torch had closed and there were few other clubs around, now stopped going.

This is the point at which accusations of elitism arise. After all, what could the objective difference be between an individual who went to Northern Soul clubs before the 1974/5 watershed and one who started to go afterwards? Those who allege elitism would argue that the putative elitists believe there was something better about the scene in its pre-1975 condition and that this belief is based on nothing of substance and is misguided. It's a fair point, but I think there is something genuine and more subtle going on which is worthy of exploration. However, here, I want to talk about the decline of the scene; an examination of these attitudes will come later, in the Wigan Casino and Mouldy Oldies sections. Whatever the case, it is true that a huge influx of new, generally younger people arrived – mostly at the doors of Wigan Casino, where busloads would be disgorged late on a Saturday night – and this changed things. If the clubs had been packed previously with a small, knowledgeable crowd, there was now a much larger crowd, content to be fed

Wigan's diet of sub-Gene Pitney, white 60s pop. And whereas many would see through this, many did not, and the large number of people who on social media still list records by Wayne Gibson, Muriel Day, Wigan's Ovation and the rest as their favourite 'Soul' tunes is instructive, as is the apparent obliviousness of many to the drug scene. Many of the earlier attendees moved on to other clubs. I was one such. My last trip to Wigan Casino was in 1976. The views of many who now opted for the Cleethorpes Pier and Winter Gardens All-Nighter, The Ritz All-Dayer in Manchester, and Blackpool Mecca, in place of Wigan Casino, are well summed up in the words (paraphrased) of that curmudgeonly Midlander, mentioned above: 'I wasn't travelling 80 miles to listen to crap like that'.

In short, by 1975, Northern Soul had ceased to be anarchic, obscure, bottom-up or indifferent to mainstream music fads. It was a mainstream fad. Within what was left of the scene, the refusal to have anything to do with influence or leadership from record companies was over, as Northern Soul became the target for sales campaigns and new, copyist music. Many records that had been exquisitely rare were now on general release. And from here developed the famous Northern Soul schism: Wigan Casino continued to develop its pop-slanted playlist, along with Soul records regurgitated from earlier clubs and its own earlier history; whilst, at the other pole of influence, Blackpool Mecca moved towards a more modern groove of new Soul and disco sounds.

This meant that both camps were diverging from Northern Soul. Wigan's playing of non-Soul of a quality that was beyond the pale and its inability to produce the volume of newly-discovered old Soul tracks meant that it was outside of what had become the Northern Soul model; but so was Blackpool Mecca, in its pursuit of the new without an ear tipped towards 'the right sound'. In the BBC's 2014 documentary on Northern Soul, Living for the Weekend, Ian Levine talked about the way his playlists went from this point.[20] He acknowledged that, through hurt and pique at the way his music choices had been received and the personal abuse he had been subjected to, he went too far, stretching the sound as far as possible from Northern Soul as a gesture of rebuke.

I would argue that Northern Soul could have survived as something other than a revivalist scene had things not got so entrenched and had the original pattern been followed; i.e.: new records with the right sound could have been carefully chosen, along with recordings that had been missed when first released but re-discovered a couple of years on. Putting it another way, if music

---

[20] BBC Living for the Weekend (2014) [online] Available on YouTube: https://www.youtube.com/watch?v=_jHx4AoCk4k [Accessed 11 January 2018]

from up to and including 1970 was played in 1970, music from up to and including 1980 could have been played in 1980, music from up to and including 1990 could have been played in 1990, and so on.[21] This is not to argue that the much-loved '60s sound' would necessarily have continued or that the same sound was available in later records (though there are and continue to be new recordings that emulate the sound); my argument is that some forward movement – some modernisation – of the sound was, before this point, part of the scene, and, as long as inappropriate tracks were avoided, new music could have been assimilated. This point is demonstrated by the popularity on the Northern Soul scene of tracks like Gil Scott Heron's 'The Bottle', The Commodores' 'The Zoo' and several All Platinum/Stang tracks (the Moments, Chuck Jackson at el). These were amongst many new records, recorded and played in the early/mid 70s, which had a very different sound from that of the 1960s, but still the 'right sound', and were massive everywhere, including Wigan. Later great records, like Idris Muhammad's 'Could Heaven Ever Be Like This', Al Hudson's 'Spread Love', George Benson's 'Love Ballad' and Phyllis Hyman's 'You Know How to Love Me', all played at some times in some of the divergent clubs, show where the future may have led.

What cannot have helped this state of entrenchment was the fact that the new arrivals on the scene from the mid-70s onwards, particularly at Wigan, did not experience the scene as it was before, when the new and the old were mixed. For this group, all of the records were oldies; the scene appeared defined by it, and people would now fight tooth and nail to fix it in the past. The fact that the scene had this name 'Northern Soul' meant that some fixed, if vague, concept of the music existed, and since it existed, other kinds of music had to be excluded. Whereas 'Soul' music could move along with whatever Soul artistes were doing, Northern Soul had a fixed identity which could not change. Its terminal decline from being a vital, progressive scene was assured. The fact that from 1976 Wigan Casino started to run 'oldies allnighters' is instructive: Northern Soul had turned back onto itself.

Things were further disrupted by a 'disco' scene that was coming to have its own particular characteristics at the same time as producing things that sounded right at Northern Soul clubs. Isaac Hayes' 'Disco Connection' and George Benson's 'Supership' are two of many tracks that were both 'disco' and major Northern Soul spins. Chic's output would have made good Northern Soul material, if it did not have so obvious home in 'disco'. This blurring of lines did not help Northern Soul's survival. Northern Soul was compelled to reject the music that would have saved it.

---

[21] The odd later track was played, but the overall trend was to look backwards, this reaching its extreme in the early noughties, when late-50s/early60s RnB started to be played on the scene.

Another, less talked about, agency was acting on the scene from outside. From the start, Northern Soul, with its skinhead associations and outsider outlook, was hard and on the edge, but from 1976, and especially by 1977, punk had stolen that ground. Northern Soul, in its baggy pants and with its outmoded attitudes, was starting to look distinctly out of place.

Taking all of this into account, we can say that from 1975 Northern Soul as we knew it was largely over, except as a regurgitating, revivalist scene. Nostalgic 'anniversary' events started to crop up, with specially designed badges, showing the dates and proving you went. The popularity of Timi Yuro's 'It'll Never be Over For Me' and the progression of those words onto endless badges and T-shirts seem to encapsulate the defiance of a rear-guard desperately trying to hold onto something that was slipping away. It is fair to say, however, that some aspects of the scene survived for another few years in less well known but more enlightened clubs than Wigan Casino, such as Cleethorpes Pier and Winter Gardens, and Manchester's Ritz, which eliminated the worst excesses of both the Wigan and the Blackpool camps and played good 'old' Soul and the best of the new, as indeed the original Northern Soul scene always had.

I need to be clear, here, that in talking about revivals and resurgences, I am not suggesting that, as some believe, the scene died out in the late-1970s and was reborn in about 2000. Although it is true that it has waxed and waned in popularity and that even Wigan Casino sometimes played to half-empty halls toward the close of the 70s, the scene never vanished completely. So when I talk about revivals, I mean that the scene mutated into a revivalist scene whilst in progress, due to defining itself around a particular style and era of Soul music and refusing to modernise. But I also make a point of saying that the scene in its original modernising and renewing mould had gone: the Northern Soul scene was over; a revival or facsimile of the Northern Soul scene persisted. And when I talk about resurgences, I refer to moments when, after a period of relative anonymity, the scene has once again caught the public eye and attracted more people – newcomers and returnees – and has expanded in terms of numbers of venues, sales of discs and memorabilia etc., and general visibility.

In summary, Northern Soul reached its defining shape in 1968-70. The end began in 1974, as Northern Soul went over ground and fragmented into various different camps that no longer had its defining characteristics, though here and there it struggled on to about 1977. I acknowledge that places like Yate and Wigan Casino itself carried on for a few more years and just into the 80s, but this was by now a revivalist scene. It did not have those vital renewing characteristics of that late-60s/early-70s scene. I also acknowledge that

Northern Soul is bigger now than it has ever been, but it is also characterised by old music, when the original scene played new and relatively recent black American music, plus some blue-eyed Soul that fitted the bill.

*The author Stalybridge, Greater Manchester, 1976, with more or less all that mattered to me at that time: Manchester United represented by the scarf, my collection of Northern Soul records at my side, and the girl behind the camera. Note the wallpaper/curtain combination. This was not a time or place where a perfectly good pair of curtains would be chucked out, just because they clashed violently with the wallpaper.*

Stafford is an interesting curiosity. It started in the 80s, as Yate and Wigan finished, and ran for four years. However, in proffering '6Ts' ('sixties') music, with some new music played in other rooms, it was already presenting itself as focused in the past with 'modern' Soul as a distinctly different entity. This foreshadowed a practice now common in large venues, where Northern Soul and Modern Soul are played in different rooms, affirming the notion that

*Northern Soul in the South: Yate Leisure Centre, near Bristol, circa 1976. Photo credit: Gillian Scott Moore*

'Northern' Soul ended in about 1975 and that music made after that date cannot be called Northern Soul and has to be called something else. The 100 Club in London started to put on Northern Soul or 6Ts nights from the end of the 1980s and was at the start of a revival that grew throughout the 1990s, presaging the broad revivalist scene we have now, and it is still going at the time of writing.

As with most youth cults, one of the key factors in bringing about the end of the original scene was the fact that those involved were growing up and moving on. Even though new people were coming along to take their places, they wanted the scene their predecessors had had, and this meant that the scene was now consciously focusing on music and fashions of the past and was, ironically, becoming ever more remote from its original values.

Northern Soul has undergone many resurgences since, as those who had left the scene to get on with adult life dusted off their dancing shoes and started seeking out Soul events in middle-age, and new people got involved. Whereas these revivals are largely characterised by nostalgia and repetition, not development and continuance, there is a 'rare and underplayed' sub-sector to the scene now, where DJs still try to unearth and play 'new' material (i.e. old records, newly discovered, or known but very rare records bought freshly to the attention of the listenership). Stafford, then the 100 Club and other places/DJs continued to source 'new' old records, but this is only one small area of a scene dominated by oldies events. It is also one that struggles because of the diminishing supply of material, and it also, arguably, has to grapple with the problem of quality, in that many would argue that the best records were skimmed off the top and played out decades ago.

Some argue that there are now two Northern Soul scenes: the rare-and-underplayed one and the oldies one. I would argue there are three: the two aforementioned and an out-and-out populist one, which doesn't only play just oldies, but confines itself to the most well-known few dozen oldies. I have been to events where records like Girls are Out to Get You, Seven Days Too Long, The Snake, Do I love You, What, Tainted Love, At the Top of the Stairs, Ain't Nothing but a House Party, Out on the Floor, The Night and There's a Ghost in My House were played over and over again. A live band – a Northern Soul 'tribute' act – doing cover versions of the best known Northern Soul tunes, is also not an unusual feature at this kind of event.

What all of these different kinds of Northern Soul event have in common, however, is that they all play records which are many times older than the ones played on the original scene – they are all revivals of a sort. Perhaps the best way to understand the difference between the scene back in the day and the one that exists now is that the one that emerged in the late-60s played records that were between brand-new and 3 or 4 years old, whilst the current scene plays records that are between forty-odd and fifty-odd years old. And whereas this means the music is more or less the same, the cultural significance of the scene then, compared to the scene now, is radically different: the original scene was constantly on the move, elusive and cutting-edge; the current one is venerable, understood and nostalgic.

## Northern Soul was a response to the wretchedness of 70s working-class life, wasn't it?

There have been several Northern Soul documentaries that make this point, and it is a seductive idea, but I am not sure it stands close scrutiny. Whereas it is the case that most people who went to Northern Soul clubs were working class, the fact is that most working-class people did not go to Northern Soul clubs. In fact, most working-class people back in the day didn't know what Northern Soul was.

It was always the case that many working-class people in tedious or back-breaking jobs would choose to restore their sanity by going crazy at weekend, but that could take many forms. As I was making my way to The Moon or The Torch or The Pendulum, Stalybridge's Greasers were head-banging to Status Quo, Deep Purple and Suzi Quatro; the local hippies were getting stoned and listening to Soft Machine, Yes and Steve Hillage; and the mainstream were getting pissed and hitting each other with pint pots in the Talbot, to a backcloth of Mud, Alvin Stardust and the New Seekers.

The same logic could also be used to explain the practice, routine in the 70s, of having a skin-full at Saturday lunchtime then heading off to the football for a punch-up.

When I started work in 1971, I was one of 30 or so new Apprentice Gas Fitters or Technicians who rolled-up, thirsting for knowledge, at Stretford Training Centre, but I was the only one into Northern Soul. I became friends with a colleague who was into contemporary mainstream Soul – Marvin Gaye, Al Green and such – and who, as a result of our friendship, also got into Northern Soul (as, later, did his brother). However, we were surrounded by young people from various bits of Manchester, Liverpool, West Yorkshire, Cheshire and Lancashire who had no interest in Northern Soul, wouldn't have even known of its existence were it not for my friend and I eulogising it, and found our interest in it a matter of some amusement. Favoured acts were the likes of Thin Lizzy, David Bowie, Elton John, Rod Stewart and even the Carpenters. (It was not particularly unfashionable to be middle-aged at 18 in the early 1970s – several of my fellow apprentices were married).

So, if most working-class people were not drawn to Northern Soul, it cannot be just working-class life that motivated those who did join the scene. There have to be other ingredients in this, and I believe there are two.

Firstly, I think the scene still carried some of the factors that motivated Mods and those who attended the early, proto-Northern Soul clubs: it promised 'cool'. There was a fashion-consciousness about the scene, in terms of its attitudes and actual clothing. It was OK to have a long bath before going out, and to shave carefully, blow-dry your hair, spray under your arms, then pick out your coolest clothes and splash on a bit of Yardley Black Label. At the other end of the spectrum, where bike-chain grease under the fingernails and looking like you've slept in the park were badges of honour, all that narcissism would have been rejected out of hand (even if the 'I don't care what I look like' look was sometimes carefully cultivated). As for the mainstream, they seemed to see fashion and music as parts of life that had to be met, dealt with and maybe enjoyed to a degree en route to proper adulthood, but they were seldom obsessions.

Secondly, there were the attractions within the characteristics of the scene itself: the fact that it was underground, obscure, quasi-illegal and had this great music, which was itself exotic through its rarity.

What you have, therefore, is a scene that satisfies the needs only of that small part of working-class society that values these things, that wants to be a part of something on the margins. It felt special to be part of the Northern Soul scene. Clearly, others wanted to be part of the latest big thing, whatever that was, and it is the case that many people from the mainstream, who were wearing flares and platform-soled boots and listening to Glam Rock, saw themselves as cutting-edge and us as strange, marginal freaks. And that was fine by us, as we saw them as undiscerning and credulous recipients of whatever television told them they should like.

I feel, also, there was another, overarching, factor to be considered in this: that 1970s working-class life might seem woeful from the outside and from a distance in time, but when you were in it, it was just life itself, and it was fine. It is often said that people who are poor and are surrounded only by other people like themselves don't recognise their circumstances, because this is just how life is. Even if it is a curiosity now, 1970s working-class life was normality for 1970s working-class people, and there wasn't the sense that 'this is so awful that I have to react against it with what I do at weekend', beyond the fact that it was normal for everyone to want to let their hair down when the week's work was done, as they always had. In fact, contrary to the various histories of the 1970s, which define it as a dreadful decade of strikes, power cuts and IRA bombings, it felt to me and my friends as a time of great excitement, colour and optimism. As now, there were new cars, new gadgets and new ideas, as well as music, fashion, football, friends and good times. Indeed, compared to the 1960s, the 70s saw a substantial rise in living standards for working-class people. If, in the 1960s, a northern, working-class family might choose between Blackpool, Southport and Rhyl for their annual summer holiday, by the end of the 1970s it was not unusual for them to jet off to the Costa Brava or Majorca. To be alive then felt like it feels to be alive now. From a personal perspective, speaking as someone who has by now parked himself in some obscure, arty part of the middle class and only gets his hands dirty while gardening, I still love Northern Soul and its clubs every bit as much as I did when I was a working-class seventeen-year-old.

There is also the matter of strata within classes. Whereas most people I went to Northern Soul clubs with were working class, most were the smarter ones, who'd made it to the grammar school or done well enough at the secondary modern to land a half-decent job. Plus there were one or two lower-middle-class people – usually sons and daughters of parents who ran their own businesses – but they were part of the same milieu because they lived and socialised in the midst of the same community. We were the ones who became skilled and semi-skilled workers, as opposed to lackeys and labourers; some eventually made it into white-collar jobs; one or two even stayed on at school, did 'A'-Levels and went on into Higher Education, though on making that transition those individuals usually left Northern Soul behind, along with their working-class communities. For any of us, joining the 'other side' and becoming a greaser was inconceivable. The Mods v Rockers prejudices persisted: we saw them as dim, unwashed low-life; they saw us as perfumed ponces. If that kind of characterisation seems uncomfortably aggressive in our times, that is part of what this book is about: to remind us of the more shamelessly aggressive attitudes that existed then, amongst hormone-packed, pre-political-correctness, working-class youths. Mods were already associated with social-climbing – an issue caught beautifully in *Quadrophenia*[22], where Sting's 'Ace Face' was a perfectly turned-out peacock by night and a lowly bellhop by day – and whereas I can recall no specific urge towards joining the middle class, which as a teenager I saw as tedious, pretentious and ignorant of real life, there was something about being clean, neatly groomed and wearing cool clothes that was attractive. Not only was the unkempt greaser look an anathema to my way of being, and to that of the people I socialised

---

[22] Quadrophenia. (1979) Film. Dir. Franc Roddam

with, my employer would not have stood for it. I acknowledge that this is a brief and possibly entirely unrepresentative survey, which those of a more academic bent might like to pick up on and examine with more comprehensive research. Nevertheless, at least from the perspective of the time and place in which I came to Northern Soul, the evidence suggests that it was the smart, literate end of the working class, plus a few of the lower-middle class, that wanted what Northern Soul had to offer; or rather, it was some individuals from those groups, as others tended towards hippie-dom and many others had no truck with any youth cult. The huge influx of new people that came to Northern Soul after it went over ground in the mid-70s were to a large extent differently motivated, in that it had gone from a cool underground scene to mainstream fad, so I suspect the demographics of that group are different, but I have no evidence with which to elaborate on that, and that again would be a matter for further research.

The popularity of the scene might also be theorised through the wildness and recklessness of youth and Dionysian impulses. In a Northern Soul all-nighter you could abandon yourself to the ecstatic fusion of drugs, dancing and music, with no thought for tomorrow. And even if people, famously, didn't dance with each other at Northern Soul clubs, that doesn't mean they didn't get together off the dancefloor. Thus, all manner of sensual pleasures were satisfied via Northern Soul. But then again, sex, drugs and music were hardly exclusive to the Northern Soul scene, so there has to be something about the particularity of the experience that attracted some and not others.

The concept of 'Bomb Culture'[23] has been posited to explain many youth cults of the era: with our illustrious leaders evidently convinced that the only answer to political annihilation was worldwide nuclear annihilation, alternative values, nihilism and escapist activities seemed more than reasonable. But again, whilst everyone was aware of the threat of nuclear destruction, it did not, in reality, impinge on daily lives or lifestyle choices. This is echoed in contemporary life: we live, now, with the threat and the growing reality of climatic disaster, but although we sit through a nightly news-time diet of floods, landslips and raging forest fires, and probably try to do our bit by half-heartedly putting out our refuse in its various recycling categories, we do not live as though ecological Armageddon is about to befall us. And the same applied then: we did not go to Northern Soul clubs because nuclear doom hung over us; we went because it was an enjoyable thing to do and one that fulfilled various needs.

Class issues might also be cited in the empathy felt by some Northern Soul fans for black Americans subjected to segregation and other forms of dis-

---

[23] Nuttall, Jeff. Bomb Culture. McGibbon and Key, London. 1968

crimination in various US states; this being expressed through the appropriation of the black fist symbol. For more on this see the chapter 'What was the appeal of Northern Soul?'. However, class-consciousness and solidarity had precious little to do with what went on in Northern Soul clubs, where the euphoric combination of music, dancing and amphetamine obliterated all other considerations.

If Northern Soul was a response to the woes of working-class life, then it was only one of many forms of expression of that impulse, and a minor one at that. The compulsion was more likely an echo of the Mod inclination towards social climbing (real or imagined) and narcissism, expressed through cool attitudes and the wearing of cool clothes, and of being part of an obscure, outsider scene with its own private obsessions. There was also the fact that the Northern Soul all-nighter and amphetamine made an irresistible combination: the drug made dancing and the music even more ecstatic and it kept you going all night, and whilst the regular clubs knocked-off at 2am, the Northern Soul all-nighter's opening hours matched the duration of the enjoyable part of the drug's effects. The appeal of Northern Soul was not just a response to the negative experience of working-class life; it was to all the positives that the scene offered – legal and otherwise, and regardless of whether others would see them as positives – and to the specific attributes of the scene that could not be found anywhere else.

# There were no drugs, right?

No drugs? You've got to be kidding me!

Drug use at Northern Soul events is one of the most controversial areas in current debates on social media. There are frequent, rather pious, interjections by individuals who say they didn't use drugs; they 'got high on the music'. That evangelism often extends to the expressed belief that because they didn't use drugs, no-one else did. Sometimes, there might be the begrudging acceptance that there may have been drugs, but it will be added that they were a minority interest. Quite how someone squares the idea that they were oblivious to drug use with a clear understanding of what proportion of revellers were taking drugs is never explained.

There are those who say, 'I never saw any drugs' (hence, there weren't any). Others say, 'I wasn't offered any drugs', as though not being offered drugs equates to clear evidence that no drugs were present. Both of these arguments are facile bits of 'logic' that any reasonably savvy child would see through. The fact is, there was a huge demand for drugs and getting your hands on them was hard work. They were also, of course, illegal. So the idea that someone would be wantonly waving drugs around, so that non-partakers could be kept informed that they were there, is absurd; as is the notion that someone would be randomly distributing drugs (for free!) to people who didn't want them.

This kind of illogical, ill-informed denial flies in the face of heaps of evidence of all kinds, from numerous personal testimonies, to police activity, to news coverage of the times. Drug use was a fundamental part of the Northern Soul scene, and most who went in its heyday either dabbled or got serious with drugs – more on this below. I will make the case for the presence of drugs by listing various issues that are in the public domain, then outlining my personal experience.

If you were around at the time, the presence of 'gear' as it was then called – speed in various forms – was palpable. Arrangements would be made before all-nighters to buy and sell. I have even bought drugs from a famous Northern Soul DJ. At the all-nighters themselves, not much visibly changed hands, because there was the possibility of being caught by members of the drug squad, but occasionally things did, and I did once see a discarded syringe in the toilets at The Torch. The thing to do was to swallow your gear just before you went into a place, so you carried nothing and turned on just as you got in. That all this went on was an open and normal aspect of being involved in the scene. That the police placed check-points on the road to the Cleethorpes all-nighter indicates their awareness of this. Inside the clubs, it was obvious who had indulged: the enlarged pupils, frantic chewing and 'speedy' mannerisms gave it away, as did, sometimes, the panic attacks during come-downs (variously referred to as 'the horrors' or 'cracking up').

People whose experience of the scene dates back as far as the dawn of The Twisted Wheel in 1963, and others from the later 60s and into 70s, talk freely on social media about having gear, stashing it, taking it, being off their heads, coming down, getting nicked, even screwing chemist shops. Others talk about their favourite types of speed, and some post pictures of pills and capsules, expressing the kind of wistful sentiment you might about a lost teenage love.

The Wheel was well-known as a place where drug use was rife. It was the target of police raids and sensational newspaper headlines about drug-addled teenagers. The reason it closed was that the police objected to its licence being renewed, because of drug use. Roger Eagle, that early driving force in the development of the club, threw in the towel as far back as 1967 because he was fed up of amphetamine-fuelled punters demanding ever faster records, and of having to ring ambulances for those who'd misjudged their ability to handle a pocket-full of purple hearts.

On the BBC's 2014 story of Northern Soul, Living for the Weekend, Peter Stringfellow, talked about his Mojo Club in Sheffield – which ran from 1964-67 and, apart from a dalliance with psychedelic music, was arguably Yorkshire's answer to The Twisted Wheel – and described, without hesitation, punters dancing all night after taking blueys and bombers.[24]

The Torch was also targeted by police because of drug use, and like the Wheel, its licence was revoked.
Wigan Casino, likewise, was the object of intense police attention and scandalised local media reports. There are numerous accounts of drug use, in-

---

[24] BBC Living for the Weekend (2014) [online] Available on YouTube: https://www.youtube.com/watch?v=_jHx4AoCk4k [Accessed 11 January 2018]

cluding the police themselves complaining in the papers that nearly everyone in the place was off their head. There is also actual footage of people arriving at and dancing in Wigan Casino. If you know what someone on speed looks like, you can tell instantly who has imbibed, and it was a fair few. In an item written in 2013, Paul Mason, now a well-known journalist, then (1975) a young Wigan-goer, describes eating an ephedrine inhaler as a substitute for speed and goes on to say: "contact with speed dealers then was expensive and dangerous: the scene was crawling with plainclothes drug squad. In the early 70s the Soul scene had been fuelled by pharmaceutical speed, stolen from chemist shops. But as drugs were withdrawn even from prescription, and the shops made more secure, 'backstreet' amphetamine sulphate powder came onto the market."[25] This was true. Demand had driven up the price and, as mentioned above, few were foolish enough to carry gear on their person inside the clubs.

To my personal experiences: bearing in mind I am talking about an illicit activity and referring to other people, who may not wish be mentioned in this context, I will be circumspect.

When I think of people I knew who went to the Soul clubs before the scene went over ground – up to and including about 1974 – about 60 or 70 names come to mind, from close friends to individuals whom I knew only as nodding acquaintances or by sight. Of those, all but handful took 'gear'. Some may have tried it once or twice; others were weekend ravers, holding-down sensible jobs during the week; others became heavy-duty drug users; some died. Had drugs not been part of the Northern Soul scene, as some claim, I might never have had cause to become familiar with the following official and slang terms: uppers, downers, dex, blueys, purple hearts, chalkies, Tenuate Dospan, Bustaids, Daprisal, just 'daps', Benzedrine, Dexedrine, amphetamine sulphate, just 'sulphate', Ritalin, ephedrine, cocaine, just 'coke', Charlie, heroin, just 'h', Skag, pirellis, Preludin, Drinamyl, Durophet, Duromine, Diconol, Palfium, Physeptone, Methadone, methedrine, green and clears, red and browns, green and browns, black bombers, white bombers, black and whites, Riker, SK&F, Filon, morphine, just 'morph', dope, Bob Hope, skunk, oil, black, hash, marijuana, cannabis, leb, whacky baccy, Billy Whizz, just 'whizz', back-street blueys, Stelladex, Lysergic Acid Diethylamide, just 'LSD', just 'acid', purple haze, lettuce, microdot, DF118s, mescaline, Pethedine, just 'peth', Nepenthe, Opium Tincture, Nembutal, works, spike, O-D, horrors, cracking-up, throwing a whitey, turning blue, magic mushrooms, psilocybin, Mogadon, just 'moggies', Mandrax, just 'mandies', Tuinal, barbiturates, just

---

[25] Mason, Paul 23 Sept. 2013 Poor-Man's Speed: Coming of Age in Wigan's Anarchic Northern Soul Scene [online] Available: http://www.vice.com/en_uk/read/northern-Soul-revival-wigan-casino-paul-mason [Accessed 23 May 2016]

'barbs', Sodium Amytal, Omnopon-Scopolamine, speedball, Temazepam, Valium, Diazepam, Librium, Ativan, benzodiazepines...

Speed was the drug of choice for Northern Soul fans, because it kept you energised and awake at the all-nighters. Only a proportion of the drugs listed above are speed. Others are drugs that might have been taken to ease the come-down after speed, which could be really nasty. Others are drugs that some graduated onto after getting started on speed at Northern Soul clubs. Some individuals handled it and came out the other end as well-balanced adults, little or no worse for the experience. Others started out like Sting's 'Ace Face' in *Quadrophenia* and ended up like Ewan McGregor's 'Renton' in *Trainspotting*.[26] The number of kids I knew back then who died directly or indirectly due to drug use approaches double figures. One of my closest friends – more like a brother, really, and someone I'd known since we were little more than toddlers – died of an accidental overdose, only a few weeks out of his teens. Without mentioning names, in order to save families hurt, these are the drug-related deaths among people I knew. The circumstances of their deaths are 'to the best of my knowledge', as detail is limited by the understandable difficulty of getting hold of specifics when such a thing happens:

A – accidental barbiturate overdose
B – accidental barbiturate overdose
C – accidental Palfium overdose
D – suicide in police cells
E – accidental heroin overdose
F – stopped breathing after taking heroin and morphine after drinking
G – left outside of A&E after overdose; died before he could be revived
H – killed in car crash, being pursued by police
I – heroin overdose – allegedly murdered by being wilfully supplied with full-strength heroin when most on the market is severely cut

I could add to these the names of several individuals whose deaths in middle age were the result of conditions which stemmed from drug use in their teens, and at least one who became and is still a hopeless addict, living on prescription methadone.[27] I have to say, on a personal note, that having seen all this, it very much rankles to be told by people who really do not know what they are talking about, that the Northern Soul scene was a drug-free affair.

It would be futile and a tedious read if I were to list, one after another, the many nights we necked our gear, went to this or that club, danced all night, then went back to Stalybridge and did our best to ameliorate our comedowns with a trip to the park to chill out, or with a substantial quantity of beer, or

---

[26] Quadrophenia. (1979) Film. Dir. Franc Roddam; Trainspotting (1996) Film. Dir. Danny Boyle
[27] I regret to have to add that during the process of writing this book, this person has died too.

a tab of acid, or all of the above. So I will just relate one tale: a car-load of us, with my mate, J, at the wheel, set off for Blackpool Mecca. We had done well for gear and each had 10 Dex and 12 Filon, which we topped up later with 8 Tenuate Dospan, scored, unusually, inside the club. By 2 in the morning we were about as off our heads as anyone at an all-nighter could hope to be. However, Blackpool Mecca chucked out at 2am, so we had to get in the car and go home. Quite why we didn't head over to Wigan Casino at this point is a matter lost to history, though I suspect it was that because we had, by this point, run out of money. Amphetamine is not normally a hallucinogen. However, if you have enough of it, and if you are tired, and if it is dark, things can sometimes happen, and J was having trouble with randomly appearing trees. Possibly as a consequence of this, we got lost in Blackpool and couldn't seem to find our way out. We then drove straight across a roundabout, which J, distracted by all those trees, had not seen. This wasn't one of those slightly raised mini-roundabouts; it was a full-sized one with high, steep edges, made from upturned flagstones, and a grass dome in the middle. One wing of the ageing Austin Cambridge was quite severely damaged, but not enough to stop the car working, and a hub cap had rolled off down the road. I can't remember if we found it, and in the circumstances we didn't want to stick around and draw the attention of the police. For the rest of the journey, J continued to do the steering and gear changing, but we were all involved in watching the road and where we were on it, and advising which trees were real and which were not.

The effects of the drugs themselves are not the only evidence of drug use; there is also the other activity that goes on around them, notably the actions of the police.

I was at the weekly Northern Soul night at Druffies in Dukinfield during one police raid. A few plain-clothes police officers had been hanging around the place for perhaps half an hour. You could always tell them – they never got the clothes right. Then, suddenly, the place filled with police – plain-clothes and uniformed – the lights went on, the doors were sealed and everyone was searched and had their arms checked for track marks.

I arrived at a friend's house one Friday night, en route to some Soul do or other, only to be greeted by a member of the drug squad, who dragged me in and included me in the raid that was under way in the house.

The drug squad raided my house. I wasn't there; it was a Saturday morning and I had overtime, but the friend I shared with, plus another who had slept over and another who had called round ready to go the United match that afternoon, were. All were greeted by the police on first-name terms. They asked where I was, also by my first name.

Many people I know – friends and more distant acquaintances – were busted by the police for possession. Several went to prison.

The trend now is for drug users to be seen, to an extent, as victims. In the 1970s, they were not. The police saw working-class drug users as the scum of the earth and behaved accordingly. Getting nicked would generally involve being beaten-up in the cells. One local police station had an officer known as 'The Beast', who was reputed to have a pathological hatred of what he saw as 'junkies' and would take great pleasure in beating-up any scrawny Tameside teenager who landed in the cells on suspicion of drug abuse.

I could write so much more on this: about the observed effects, long and short term, of drug use on different individuals; the highs and lows; the mental, spiritual and physical torments and degradations – dragging your overdosed mate around town in the middle of the night, to stop him drifting into sleep and possibly on into a more permanent form of oblivion, was the least of it – but that would be another book. The point here is not to excavate that kind of detail, but to emphasise the point that this all went on, to counter the 'there were no drugs' myth. It is worth emphasising, also, that this is just some of what I saw, in and around my little bit of Greater Manchester; it could be equally mapped out onto the lives of countless others, in other towns, cities and suburbs across the Midlands and North of the UK.

The notion that the authentic 1960s-through-to-70s Northern Soul scene was drug-free or that drugs were only a minority interest is utterly wrong and is one of the major myths that needs to be dispelled. Amphetamine use was as much a part of the Northern Soul scene as Ecstasy was to the Acid House/Rave scene, though, of course, it was not obligatory and not everyone partook. We can only speculate why some people perpetuate the myth that there were no drugs. On the one hand, there may be those who know there was drug use, don't like it, and wish to reinvent the scene on their terms. Certainly, there is a tone of self-righteous indignation in the comments of this sort on social media. On the other, there are evidently those who really did not know what was going on around them. There may also be those who were only peripherally exposed to the scene and in their limited experience, there were no drugs around.

Expanding on those thoughts: one can imagine that people who were teenagers then and are middle aged or older now, with responsibilities and kids of their own, would not wish to be associated with drugs or with anything that might justify their own kids experimenting with drugs. But it must also be the case that many people genuinely did not take drugs and some did not see drugs being used. This could be for various reasons. I would argue that it would have been impossible for anyone deeply involved in the scene before it went over ground in about 1975 not to have been aware of drug use. The huge influx of new people from 1975 seems, however, to have changed things. Some newcomers joined in and behaved just as those already there did, i.e.: they got involved, made contacts and took drugs, but others didn't. I mentioned, above, that, of the people I knew on the scene before 1974, the vast majority took drugs. However, when I think of friends who started to go after that point, a much smaller proportion indulged, though all were aware of drugs and most had friends who took them.

What also seems to have happened is that, of the large number of people who arrived from 1975, many did not immerse themselves in the scene to the extent that they became aware of drug use, at all. Among the large numbers who arrived in those famous Wigan coach parties, there must have been many who only went once or twice, never went to any other clubs, and really did not grasp the culture that surrounded them. Certainly it is the case that, whilst many histories of Northern Soul talk elegiacally about the frantic, skilful activity on Wigan Casino's dancefloor, few mention the large numbers who surrounded the dancefloor, flat out, fast asleep. Clearly, this group had not touched any amphetamine and, in their comatose state, they would not have seen anyone take it either. They would also not have learned to recognise what a speeding person looks like. Moreover, after spending their pocket money on such a long, arduous trip, only to spend the night sleeping fitfully and uncomfortably, slumped over a table, they might not have gone back for more, and would never have come to terms with the full complexity of Northern Soul culture. Others, once Northern Soul had been popularised, might never have gone to an all-nighter and have only been exposed to the music at local clubs, youth clubs or via mates' or older siblings' turntables. Clearly, this group would also have been unlikely to have been exposed to drug use.

There is also the matter of proportions. Wigan Casino was the pivotal club when Northern Soul went over ground. For many, it would have been the only club they ever went to. And it was a much bigger venue than The Torch and, especially, The Twisted Wheel. So, if 500 people, mostly off their heads, were crammed into The Torch, then we could say that a majority at The Torch took drugs. But if the same 500, still off their heads, were surrounded by 1500 wholesome, mostly drug-free newcomers at Wigan Casino, then you might reasonably say that a majority there were not on drugs.

There is also the strange matter of projection: on quizzing drug deniers about their age, it becomes apparent that some are too young ever to have attended any of the clubs from the scene's heyday on which they are holding forth. It seems that their experience of Northern Soul clubs is one of nostalgic reinvention and, within that reinvention, there are no drugs.

The recent Northern Soul movies, *Soul Boy* (2010) and *Northern Soul* (2014), both produced a large number of sanctimonious complaints on social media about their depiction of drug use.[28] Whereas both films included references to drug use as part of their narrative, the latter was most frank and accurate in its depiction of the way drugs were an integral part of the scene for many. *Soul Boy* was essentially a rather soggy and unconvincing love story, built around Northern Soul. However, many on social media liked it more because of this and because it placed less emphasis on drug use than *Northern Soul*. For those particular viewers, the standard of the film was inversely proportional to the amount of drugs depicted. The qualities that might otherwise have made *Northern Soul* the superior film could not be acknowledged because its depictions of drug use placed it beyond the pale. By extension, those individuals who reacted to it in this way wanted to send the message, through the public forum of social media, that they would have liked those films to have minimised or, better still, eliminated any references to drug use. But why would they do this, when the reality is that drugs were a major part of Northern Soul culture, and both films would have been dishonest and strangely lacking had they excluded any drug reference?

What we must be looking at here is ignorance on the part of some; a rose-coloured-specs desire to sanitise the past on the part of others; and a more general proprietorial attitude toward Northern Soul, in which people take to themselves the right to rewrite its history on terms that better suit their outlook in older age. But, whatever the motivating impulse, all of these positions contribute to a pressure to create and hold in place the myth that the Northern Soul scene was a drug-free affair. I should add, however, that these revisionist views placed on social media were shouted down by many other contributors, who knew and told the truth.

---

[28] Soul Boy. (2010) Film. Dir. Shimmy Marcus; Northern Soul. (2014) Film. Dir. Elaine Constantine

## There was no violence or bad behaviour; it was all sweetness and light, all S.O.U.L. – Sounds Of Unity and Love – wasn't it?

E r, no, that's not true either. As with the drug issue, there has been a re-imagining on the part of some of the part violence and crime played in Northern Soul.

Northern Soul emerged in working-class Britain, and British working-class culture has a long history of violence, be that in the form of football riots, punch-ups in pubs, glassings in clubs, or tussles for dominance on the street, in the work place, in the home and elsewhere. Urban street violence has been around for as long as there have been urban streets. Gang culture is part of this, from the Peaky Blinders, Scuttlers and Sloggers of the nineteenth and early twentieth centuries, to the Teddy Boys, Mod, Rockers, Skinheads and so on of the later twentieth century. Gang culture persists to this day in Britain's inner cities.

Northern Soul emerged from the Mod scene, before making its way via the Skinhead and Suedehead scenes to the form in which it is now best known. All of these sub-cultures have violent associations. Sensationalist reportage highlighted mostly their violent aspects in order to sell papers and give the curtain-twitching, 'it shouldn't be allowed' brigade something to be outraged, censorious and vicariously thrilled about. I would not want to emulate that, and I hope in what follows I will give a balanced account that is both frank about bad behaviour on the scene, whilst placing it in context and recognising that the scene overall was pretty well behaved. I will start by listing some personal experiences and will develop my arguments from there.

As set out above, my first Soul club was The Moon in Dukinfield. I started going there in 1969, the year Skinheads became the most visible youth cult. I was a Skinhead, as was nearly every other male who went to The Moon.

The girls mostly wore the Mod look of mini-skirt or mini-dress; some wore the female adaptation of the Skinhead look. As time passed, we became Suedeheads and Smoothies, which were more or less halfway between Skinheads and Mods in style. My interest in these youth cults was to do with the fashion. I liked the look, the vague sense of belonging to something, and the feeling that the fashion notionally meant you looked hard, even if, like me, you weren't. I hasten to add that I had no truck with the racism that went with the territory and was shocked and confused by that aspect when I became cognisant of it: how could I love Desmond Dekker and Doris Troy whilst harbouring a desire to kick the shit out of them in the unlikely event that we ever met? How could someone's skin colour be a reason to hate them? I would say, also, that this was a view shared by all of my Skinhead friends at the time. Elsewhere, however, some individuals squared the contradiction by coming to the view that some non-white people – black ones, who had this possible connection to Soul and Reggae and were therefore possibly cool and like 'us' – were OK, while others – brown ones – were not OK, this being indicative of the absurdity at work in this overall.

What went on in lives of the many other Skinheads, whom I did not personally know, away from The Moon, I cannot say, but in The Moon there were few or no non-white people and the fighting was largely internecine – and there was a lot of it.

Sometimes the fighting seemed to be almost continuous, with skirmishes breaking out one after another in all corners of the place. Much of it was to do with gang rivalry: Haughton Green vs Hyde vs Ashton vs Clayton and so on. Then there were the 'are you lookin' at my bird?' sorts of disputes: some vague, trumped-up infringement, made up in order to have the risible ego-boost of making someone back down, or just to start a fight for no reason other than the pleasure of fighting. I never looked for trouble, but being in The Moon at all was enough to attract it.

There were stairs either side of the dancefloor, from the ground floor to the balcony. They had a little landing, as they turned at halfway, which gave a vantage point over the dancefloor. I was standing there one night, with my mate, Steve, leaning on the railing and gazing absentmindedly at the dancefloor, when someone kicked me hard in the back of the leg. I looked round to see a bunch of Harrington-clad youths, whom I knew vaguely by sight – the Denton crew, possibly. From the middle, their leader stepped forward, snarling something at me. I couldn't tell what he was saying because of the music, but I guessed it wasn't anything good – and he had just kicked me – so I unloaded a straight right into the middle of his face. He shot backwards, looking rather shocked, and was caught by his mates. Cornered, as we were on the stairs and heavily outnumbered, Steve and I tried to push past them to the relative safety of the ground floor. I hit the ground at the bottom of the stairs, under the weight of bodies and a few ineffectual kicks and punches, but the onslaught I was expecting didn't arrive, presumably because of the quick actions of the bouncers. However, the following week, a fist appeared from between a crowd of people and delivered me an equivalent straight right. It belonged, apparently, to a friend of the guy I had hit. I didn't mind. It seemed to straighten things out, and that was that. Not all of the violence was this ineffectual, however.

In one particular fight, in the days before hobnailed boots were banned, an individual I will call 'S' put the boot in so ferociously that the victim was reputed to have been within inches of his life.

There were rumours of a particularly sadistic Skinhead, whom I will call 'M', who was reputed to carry a cut-throat razor, with which he would go to work on anyone who crossed him.

Whereas fights in The Moon were usually between rival Skinhead gangs, their 'traditional' enemy was the Greaser fraternity. This was a continuance of the Mods v Rockers conflict; one given recognition at around that time by the fight between Alex and his droogs and Billy Boy and his, in *A Clockwork Orange* (1971).[29] One night a fight broke out in and around the frontage of The Moon, as a crew of Greasers arrived to confront the Skinheads inside. I had to walk my girlfriend to the bus stop, exiting from the club's front door and passing through the in-progress skirmish. As we stood at the bus stop, the Greasers retreated to in front of the pub across the road from The Moon. The two mobs then continued the fight by throwing bottles and bits of bar stool at each other, with my girlfriend and I standing in the middle, under an arc of flying wood and glass, eagerly awaiting the bus.

One night, whilst on the balcony at The Moon, I witnessed three members of what I took to be the same Denton mob, mentioned above, confronting an individual from Dukinfield, whom I vaguely knew and will call 'G'. They really had picked on the wrong guy. Two of them were seated, precariously and stupidly, on the balcony's edge, whilst the other got in G's face. As a means of conflict resolution, G grabbed the seated pair by their Harringtons, pulling both together in one not-insubstantial fist, and explained to the third that if he didn't back off, his friends would be taking a rapid, vertical trip to the ground floor.

On busy nights, when the numbers merited it, the management of The Moon

---

[29] A Clockwork Orange (1971) Film. Dir. Stanley Kubrick

laid on a late-night bus to take revellers back to their various bits of Pennine East Manchester. Hardly surprisingly, fights that had started in the club continued on board. One night, despairing at the mayhem going on behind him, the driver switched from his normal route and piloted his double-decker and its contents straight to the police station for the officers to sort out.

The Moon was by no means unique in experiencing this kind of aggro. The Birdcage in nearby Ashton-under-Lyne had the same issues. Again, I saw many fights break out there. I was there on one occasion when the whole place seemed to go off like a Western saloon. Being more a lover than a fighter and having, by now, seen this so many times before, I sat it out in an alcove with my girlfriend, watching the battle go on, as you would a floor show. When it had finished, we went out to have a proper look. There was glass everywhere. The whole of the floor seemed to be carpeted in it. There was a rumour that at the height of the battle someone had been thrown off the balcony and seriously injured.

A few years later, at Druffies in Dukinfield, I was sitting at a table, chatting with two friends whom I will call J and C. At a nearby table, a lanky kid was glaring at us, evidently spoiling for a fight. J and myself were regular guys, not interested in fighting unless we were given no alternative. C, on the other hand, was one of the most ferocious fighters I have ever seen; someone no-one in their right mind would tangle with. There were numerous stories about his battles. Not only was he completely without fear, fighting was his favourite pastime. He was reputed, back in the Skinhead days, to have drop-kicked the leader of the local Greasers off his motorbike, as he idled at traffic lights. The kid did not know who he was and could not have made a worse choice. He stood up and threw a pint pot in our general direction; it hit the table close to where C was sitting. In one instant, seamless move, C left his chair, squared-up to the kid and punched him in the face three times, fast and very, very hard. I'd never seen punches that fast, that hard, outside of the professional boxing ring. The kid crumpled, evidently out on his feet, and dropped to his knees. C took a pace back, steadied himself, and launched a ferocious kick into the kid's face, with the rock-hard leading-edge of his leather-soled brogues. The kid flipped over backwards, blood and bits of face spraying in an arc above him, and was then motionless. Before C could move in for whatever he had next in mind, two big, hefty bouncers were on him. He was still trading blows with them as they bundled him out.

What does all this have to do with Northern Soul? Well, these places were proto-Northern Soul and actual Northern Soul clubs. While all this fighting was going on, beautiful Soul music was playing in the background. The Northern Soul scene, as it emerged at the end of the 60s and the beginning of the 70s, did so with the Skinhead/Suedehead scene as part of its make-up, with all that implies. The Druffies incident was probably around 1975, long after Northern Soul had gone over ground and become a clearly defined entity.

It is often said that the major clubs, like Blackpool Mecca and the all-nighters, did not experience the same behaviour. This seems to be true, but only to an extent, and I will explore possible reasons why and what actually did go on.

I didn't make it to the original, 1963-71, Twisted Wheel. I was too young – it closed just as I left school. Many of those who did go, however, talk in great detail about their experiences on social media. That the club is much loved is abundantly clear, but the idea that it was not all sweetness and light is also palpable; in particular, 'rolling' crops up time and again. 'Rolling' was the term used at that time for 'mugging', and many recall being rolled in the toilets at the Wheel. Unless you could handle yourself, you would be likely to leave the gents without your money or your watch. And, of course, if you resisted being rolled, a fight was a likely outcome.

*Dark catacombs. Pete Roberts in one of the dark, damp archways of the Twisted Wheel on Whitworth Street in Manchester in 2012. Like The Pendulum, The Wheel was subterranean. Few Northern Soul clubs in the 1970s could claim to be elegant, upmarket places. Many were really not for the faint-hearted. Photo credit: Stephen Riley, with permission of Pete Roberts/The Twisted Wheel.*

Another of Manchester's legendary Northern Soul clubs, The Pendulum, had a not-undeserved reputation for violence. In a conversation in 2012 with Pete Roberts, DJ and promoter at the current incarnation of The Twisted Wheel, we reminisced about The Pendulum, amongst other places, and Pete told me he called The Pendulum the "flat nose club", because of all the fighting that went on there. I have to admit, I have had some personal experience of what he was talking about.

On one occasion in The Pendulum, my mate walked past a group of guys who were stood chatting in a circle, one of whom, for no discernible reason, spun round and started punching him. I grabbed the bloke from behind and held him in a headlock until the bouncers arrived. That was seconds, but it seemed an eternity, and had it been any longer the bloke's mates would have been on top of me. The bouncers put themselves between my mate and I and the gang, and told us to get our coats and go, fast – they'd hold these maniacs off as long as they could to give us a head start. We grabbed our coats and ran. On another Pendulum night, a guy walked up to me on the dancefloor and menacingly – in my face, more or less nose-on-nose – asked me if I wanted to buy any gear. I thought I recognised him: if he was who I thought he was, I'd seen him kick some guy's head in, savagely, on Hyde bus station some months earlier. He'd kept on booting this guy's face long after he'd hit the ground and probably lost consciousness, kicking his head, again and again, against the concrete footings of the bus shelter. He was a fierce, wiry-looking guy, a bit like Begbie in the film *Trainspotting*. For readers who have only ever moved in safer circles than these, Irvine Welsh's monstrous psychopath isn't just a figment of an author's imagination; he is a real flesh-and-bile character, living in every inner city and godforsaken, edge-of-town council estate in the land, and he is reborn with every generation. I made the quick calculation that if said 'yes', I'd give him my money and never see it again (or any gear); but if I said 'no', I'd be a wuss and get my head kicked in. I therefore said I would like to buy some gear, but was on the dole and had no money to buy it with. It was a lie, but it seemed to wrong-foot him and he left it at that. To be on the dole in those days was still to be the object of sympathy. That was another night when we left sharpish.

A friend who is a year or so older than myself and who therefore made it to the Soul clubs sooner recalls being rolled/mugged at the Top Twenty in 1968. The Top Twenty was a Soul club contemporary to The Twisted Wheel on the outskirts of Manchester, in Hollinwood. Another friend was rolled in the toilets on his first visit to Wigan Casino. That this went on was well known, and a trip to the gents was a moment to steel yourself for a confrontation. Some rollers would take your money, then give you enough back for your bus fare home.

One night at Wigan Casino, I was in the toilets, combing the sweat-soaked hair out of my face, when a lad next to me spoke and showed me his comb. "You want to get yourself one of these, mate", he said, proffering a woman's comb, the sort with the long handle, made from aluminium, the handle having been filed into a blade with a very sharp-looking point. "Just my little insurance policy", he added. He wasn't being threatening, just showing off, I suppose. So I nodded approvingly – it didn't seem the right moment to start a debate about the sense and morality of carrying weapons in night clubs – and we went our separate ways.

One morning, as Wigan Casino was turning out after an all-nighter, I found my route to the upstairs cloakroom blocked by a group of people who had stopped at the foot of the stairs and were refusing to go up, because of some kerfuffle going on near the top. I asked what was going on. It turned out that some black kid was sat on the stairs, having the horrors, and was lashing out with an afro comb at anyone who came near him, so no-one wanted to risk climbing the stairs and going past him. I had a lift waiting, so couldn't hang around for the situation to be resolved. I sprinted up the stairs, past the tormented youth. He seemed bewildered and maybe taken by surprise, and as much immersed in his own internal misery as threatening. The comb didn't come anywhere near me. It was clear, however, that on the return journey he'd have had more chance to see me, as I picked up my sheepskin from the cloakroom and turned to make my way down. So I put the coat over my head and shoulders for protection and ran back down past him. The expected slashing at the coat never happened and I got down unscathed. C – the same C mentioned above in the fight at Druffies – had also encountered this situation, but had dealt with it in his own way. Spinning a coke bottle menacingly in his hand, he walked slowly up to the kid, saying "out of the way, n****r". I didn't witness this personally; it came up in conversation later, and I always took it that the situation C had faced was identical to the one I had. Only later did it occur to me that possibly it was C's intervention that had triggered the kid's attack of the horrors in the first place. I should add, for what it's worth, that C was one of those people from my home patch who had latched onto the scene after it had gone over ground and was not a dyed-in-the-wool Soul boy.

On my first visit to The Torch, in 1972, a friend and I took seats adjacent to an older guy, still wearing the late-Mod look and looking like a member of The Move. Possibly speeding and paranoid, he turned on us and accused us of dipping into his pockets. We moved elsewhere before the situation had chance to develop. Another friend describes seeing one guy seriously beating up another on the stairs at The Torch. "He was really creaming him", was the way he put it. Another friend had her brand-new leather coat stolen from the cloakroom at The Torch. This is hardly high-level crime, even if some of the violence was pretty nasty, but it does speak of a scene that isn't necessarily as filled with brotherly and sisterly love as some would suggest, and there were other extremes: one night at the Blue Room in Sale (a.k.a. Sale Mecca), as I was buying a drink, my attention was drawn to a small group of people standing next to me at the bar, one of whom was brandishing an automatic pistol. I have no idea what that was about or even if it was a real gun – I didn't stick around to find out. However, Tony Wilson, in his book 24 Hour Party People (2002), talks at some length about Manchester's criminal underworld and its involvement in 'protecting' clubs.

Rick and Diane (not their real names), whom I had met on the Northern Soul scene in the early 70s and been friends with throughout, were by the late 70s a married couple. One Saturday lunchtime, Rick and I went to the pub, whilst Diane and my then girlfriend went shopping. The plan was that the ladies would come to the pub and meet up with us a couple of hours later. For some reason, which I can no longer recall, there was a misunderstanding over the arranged time and they arrived about half an hour late. Rick went berserk and started punching Diane ferociously in the face. I dragged him off and held him down, but not before he'd done enough to give her a huge, ugly black eye. Some time later, when things had calmed down, I asked Rick what the hell he thought he was doing. He explained that no-one looking in from the outside could ever really understand the inner workings of a relationship between a man and a woman, and I should not interfere. As an explanation, it sounded like somewhere between the inference that some sort of tacit sado-masochistic agreement existed between them, which excused his actions, and mystical bullshit. It was by no means the first of Rick's demented rages, but it was the worst I had witnessed first-hand, and it was effectively the end of our friendship. A year or two later, I heard of Rick's death from a heroin overdose. I was saddened to hear this, but I can't say it was much of a surprise. What did come as a surprise, however, was his subsequent resurrection. Rick's outrageous behaviour extended beyond domestic violence: he had a habit of taking drugs from people with a promise to pay later; a promise that was seldom kept. Through this practice, he had accumulated quite a few enemies over the years. His apparent death had been no more than a rumour wilfully spread to get his creditors off his back, whilst he vanished from Tameside and set up home secretly somewhere on the Lancashire coast. Some months or years later I heard that Rick had died again; permanently, this time. The rumour was that, to get back at him for all those thefts, someone had deliberately him given full-strength heroin, when most of what is on the market is severely cut. He therefore took far more than he was used to and died of an overdose.

If there were violence, theft and other criminality in the pubs and clubs, there was also a good deal of it outside. Many would 'jump' the train on the way to all-nighters; others, now, talk quite openly about stealing cars to get to or back home from the clubs; and then there was the substantial criminal infrastructure necessary to provide the drugs that so many consumed at these functions.

Until the mid-70s, when back-street blueys and amphetamine sulphate started to appear, all of the drugs taken at Northern Soul clubs were prescription amphetamines. A tiny proportion of these might have been someone's mum's slimming tablets, nicked from the household medicine cabinet; others might have been procured by persuading gullible GPs to write suitable prescriptions. The rest were stolen from pharmacies, and given that we are talking about a vast quantity of drugs being stolen and consumed over a long period of time, this meant that there were a huge number of such robberies and that there was a large number of people prepared to do it. Standing back and looking at it in this way, it becomes apparent that to a large extent the Northern Soul scene was underpinned by crime. Taking these drugs was a mildly illegal activity; robbing chemist shops was a much more serious one. The wild-eyed, gum-chewing revellers at all-nighters were both high on illegal substances and receivers of stolen goods; their suppliers were thieves and pushers. It is hardly surprising, then, that the police took an interest. They weren't only trying to catch drug users; they were after robbers who were costing local pharmacies substantial sums.

This also meant that, by being involved in Northern Soul, you were potentially moving into the criminal community. For many this experience was a matter of a few brief encounters during their youth; once they had grown up and drifted away from the scene, it was over. For others, however, drug-taking became a more serious matter, and that meant full immersion into the criminal community.

A well documented spat broke out on social media which encapsulates much of what I am referring to. A woman who had only just seen the movie *Northern Soul* (2014), reacted to it by objecting to the fact that it showed violence and saying she 'NEVER' (her capitals) saw any fighting at all-nighters. One of those who responded said he'd seen brawls at The Torch that spilled out onto the street, a fight outside VaVa in Bolton and several at Wigan Casino, including one in which the bouncers came off worst. This contributor is a well-known and well-respected figure on the scene and someone I knew by sight at The Torch. He pointed out to the woman that if she'd been speeding – and the woman in question has said in other posts that she did take speed – she may well have been having an intense conversation, of the sort only speeders have, or giving it some on the dancefloor, and it would have been easy not to notice such a thing in a packed, very noisy club. Others brought up the subject of rolling, again, and talked about how prevalent it was.

I personally witnessed a brawl at Wigan Casino: I was near the back/right (as you look at the stage), of the dancefloor, when some sort of commotion broke out. There was shouting and people stopped dancing and turned to look, as a jumble of bodies and flailing arms swept urgently and awkwardly down the walkway at the left of the dancefloor toward the main entrance – presumably the bouncers showing some miscreants the door.

Another area of criminal activity associated with Northern Soul is the bootlegging of records. Though less talked about than the drug scene, it was an area of pretty intense activity. A probably unknowable but very substantial number of Northern Soul's once rare records exist as bootlegs, which have permeated the scene and found their ways into many record collections. This means that, through copyright theft, artists and record companies have been robbed of tens of thousands, maybe hundreds of thousands of pounds' worth of royalties. Views on the scene are ambivalent. For some serious record collectors, bootlegs are despised and only original vinyl will do.[30] Others are just grateful to get their hands on a record that would otherwise be completely beyond reach. Some bootlegs are pretty convincing copies of the original. On the Soul Source website,[31] serious collectors exchange tips on what tiny differences separate the original from the counterfeit, which can be as little as the bits of information scratched into the run-out strip, between the playing part of the record and the label. Some bootlegs, however, are much more blatant. A guy called Jeff King, from Leicester, pressed thirty of Northern Soul's most treasured tunes on his own Soul Sounds label at the start of the 70s.[32] Further bootlegs came out on labels such as OOTP (Out of the Past), Soul Fox and Soul Galore. And there were others.

It is also important to emphasise, here, that this is just my experience and gathered knowledge. Thousands, maybe tens of thousands, had their own equivalent experiences. And I was a fairly taciturn youth, who avoided trouble as far as possible; others were far readier to fight and much more thoroughly and enthusiastically embroiled in the criminal underworld that procured and sold the drugs that co-existed with the scene. That all adds up to a large amount of violent and criminal behaviour, in towns and cities both close to and hundreds of miles from mine. But then again, it has to be emphasised

---

[30] See also 'Rarity, Divs and Handbaggers', below.
[31] Soul Source [online] Available: https://www.soul-source.co.uk/ [Accessed 26 February 2018]
[32] Martinsbox.tripod.com Jeff Kings (sic) Thing [online] http://martinsbox.tripod.com/id60.htm [Accessed 28 May 2016]

that it must be the case that many of these individuals would have got up to mischief of some sort even if the Northern Soul scene had never existed. My point is not that the Northern Soul scene was in some way intrinsically wicked and caused all of this, that somehow dancing to Jay and the Techniques fostered violent and criminal impulses. Whilst one has to acknowledge that the scene's culture may have led some astray, it is also the case that the scene was the people in it; the people in it created and perpetuated its culture. The working-class and lower-middle-class class youths of the era, who chose the Northern Soul scene ahead of other youth cults, shaped the scene to their own preferences and by their own actions, and took from it what they wanted.

And then there is the experience of women. I have necessarily written from my own experiences and those of my, mostly male, mates. But I have seen on social media comments from women who have alluded to sexual assaults, and I knew of an individual from the scene in the early 70s who was convicted of rape. And, of course, there are women who made the transition from weekend ravers and pill-poppers to full-on junkies, like many of the males I have mentioned. An equivalent book to this, written from a woman's perspective, is, it seems to me, something that is vitally needed.

In summary: the idea that the Northern Soul scene was some sort of crime-free, drug-free, violence-free, racism-free utopia is a myth. Northern Soul emerged from Britain's working class and the Mod and Skinhead scenes, all of which have richly varied histories, in which crime and violence play a part. That isn't to say that violence and crime were relentless and visible. Much of the time events went off without incident, but some clubs – usually the provincial, local venues – could be pretty nasty at times. Quite what it was about Manchester's Pendulum that made it the "flat nose club" is not clear, though the fact that it was located in Victoria, close to and more or less bisecting inner-city slum areas of both Manchester and Salford that had fearsome reparations, may have had something to do with it. The fact that it was a dingy, underground dive bar may have also been a factor: the 'Broken Windows Theory' does suggest that seedy environments encourage anti-social behaviour. As if to prove that point, I never saw any mischief in Blackpool Mecca's well appointed Highland Room, apart from pill-popping, though maybe I just got lucky. What is true and worthy of discussion is the fact that, in general, the major clubs and all-nighters were relatively trouble-free, especially when you consider the numbers of people involved. But it has to be said that this was by no means entirely the case, as my observations above make clear. Why this is, is an interesting question. The absence of alcohol is often cited. This may be true, to a point, but some clubs did serve booze, up to the hour when licensing prohibited it, and it was not necessarily the case that a club that served alcohol would necessarily be violent, or that a booze-free allnighter would be entirely trouble-free. If the lack of booze meant that inhibitions were not broken down as they might be in a regular club, the sense of being away from home turf may have created some inhibitions. Connected to this, another possibility is that, having travelled so far and gone to so much expense, folk were not going to risk being bounced out of a club. No-one would relish the thought of being turfed out of an all-nighter and then waiting hours for trains and buses to resume on a Sunday morning, with nothing to do and nowhere to go. Another aspect is that the edginess and paranoia caused by speed created nervousness that sometimes precluded aggression. On the other hand, that same edginess could sometimes spill over into paranoid perceptions and panic-driven action. But having said all this, even at the most well-behaved Northern Soul event, a very special pair of X-ray specs, of a kind that would expose the truth about all the characters present, would be likely to reveal a substantial number of drug users, some pushers and chemist-shop burglars, fences, train-fare dodgers, car thieves, thugs, racists, shoplifters, muggers, and traders in and buyers of counterfeit products, as well as some perfectly decent, blameless people.

All of this begs the question of why the utopian myths exist. The answers must be the same as those in the drug issue: a mixture of delusional nostalgia, wilful dishonesty, forgetfulness and genuine ignorance of what was really going on. Plus, there will be those who hold opinions on the scene who weren't actually there and have formed their views through projection, secondhand anecdotes, old photographs and imagination.

# Everyone wore baggy pants and a bowling shirt, right?

On the BBC's One Show, one evening in the spring of 2014, Alex Jones and Matt Baker appeared at the start of the programme wearing very particular clothing. She wore a snug T-shirt with a circle skirt, of the sort that flares out if you spin when dancing; he wore baggy trousers with a bowling shirt. They announced that they were wearing these clothes because they had a Northern Soul feature coming up later in the show and wanted to be in the spirit of the thing by donning the right gear. Evidently they believed that this was the standard look for Northern Soul events. They are not alone in this belief. The kit they were wearing has become, in the minds of many, a kind of Northern Soul uniform.

The idea that this is the 'Northern Soul look', that these are the only outfits worn at Northern Soul venues and that everybody wore them, is not true; it is another myth. In the period we are looking at – from the late 60s to the late 70s – that look was only the fashion briefly and most certainly was not observed by everyone even then. Fashions varied widely and things changed rapidly from the start: from the male perspective alone (though the girls sometimes wore the same stuff), you had to have a Ben Sherman shirt, or a Jaytex at a pinch, with Levis or Wranglers jeans, braces and hobnailed boots; then you had to have a granddad shirt; then you had to have one black leather glove; then you had to have a parka; then you had to have a Fred Perry; then you had to have Lee Riders jeans; then you had to have Doctor Martens boots; then you had to have monkey boots; then you had to have a Lee or Wrangler or Levi blue denim jacket; then the same in white denim; then the same in pin-cord corduroy; then you had to have Lee or Wrangler or Levi cord pants; then you had to have white jeans (an impractical fad that was even shorter-lived than the others); then you had to have a long cardigan; then you had to have Royals brogues, with the pattern going in a straight line up the side – ordinary brogues didn't count; then you had to have tassel loafers; then you had to have Royals Comos; then you had to have Levi Sta-Prest pants; then you had to have KDs ('Khaki Drill': light-coloured army pants); then you had to have Tonic (or imitation Tonic) trousers; then you had to have a barathea blazer with a badge on the top pocket; then you had to have red socks; then you had to have a sleeveless jumper or tank top; then you had to have a Harrington jacket; then you had to have a whole Tonic suit, with a big split up the back of the jacket (there was a peculiar virility thing going on: your split had to be bigger than the next guy's), with a hanky carefully displayed in the top pocket; then you had to have a Crombie fly-front overcoat (or, more likely, a cheap imitation thereof); then you had to have a sheepskin coat; then you had to have Prince of Wales check trousers; then you had to have Rupert pants (basically, imitation Tonic pants with a large check pattern); then you had to have a Battenberg jumper; then you had to have Skinners jeans; then you had to have a skinny-rib jumper; then you had to have wide parallels; then you had to have a penny-round collar shirt; then you had to have a pin-tuck Simon shirt; then you had to have a pin-tuck leather jacket; then you had to have a leather bomber jacket with an elasticated waist; then you had to have baggy trousers; then you had to have duck shoes; then you had to have a V-neck T-shirt with a pointed collar, rather like the football shirts of the period; then you had to have wedge-soled shoes; then you had to have a long, double-breasted raincoat; then you had to have a long, leather 'Shaft' coat; then you had to have a pyjama-collared, short-sleeved shirt; then you had to have very baggy trousers with a high waist band and too many buttons and pockets; then you had to have a bowling shirt with some garish logo on the back, usually referencing some imaginary American diner or car repair place; then you had to have corduroy baggies; then you had to have denim baggies, with turn-ups; then you had to have a cap-sleeved T-shirt; then you had to have a cheese-cloth shirt; then you had to have Solatios or other pattern-fronted, wide, leather-soled shoes; then you had to have a short, acrylic V-neck jumper with a deep waistband and a pattern or three stars on the front; then you had to have extremely baggy trousers with a very high waistband and a nonsensical number of pockets and buttons; then you had to have a coloured vest with badges on it, telling everyone which Northern Soul clubs you'd been to (or wished you'd been to); then you had to have A-line flared trousers (not baggies or conventional from-the-knee flares – these were tight on the bum and flared from the upper-thigh all the way down); then you have to have a slim-fitting, big-collared, poly-cotton shirt with a playful repeat pattern all over; then, outside of the all-nighter's doors, punk was under way, and trousers started to narrow again and peg leg trousers started to enter the scene.

No doubt many experienced some of these fashions in a different order, and indeed, many happened concurrently. Plus, of course, an item might be kept for quite some time, so many styles persisted for a while before becoming passé.

Apologies to the ladies for not having an equivalent list of female fashions, but I was clearly concentrating more on what I was buying. Evidently, those girlfriends who accused me of being inattentive had a point.

*The author, summer 1972. It was on a weekend and I was going to or had been to The Torch – wearing that shirt, without the jumper. It was a Simon, pin-tuck, knitted-cotton shirt, with a brown, green and white flower pattern all over, and that giant, fly-away collar. As eccentric as it may seem now, it was not an unusual look then. I was also wearing Skinners jeans, which were about 24 inches at the hem and considered extremely wide at the time.*

As with any other youth cult, people at Northern Soul clubs wanted to look cool and up to date with the fashions of the moment. Much of what was worn at Northern Soul clubs reflected what was happening, fashion-wise everywhere, for people of that age group, class and income-bracket. It is also the case, however, that some Northern Soul fans tweaked fashions, by customising what they bought or by getting tailors to modify designs, by adding more pockets and buttons, for example. Though these were then copied by manufacturers, mass produced and made available to all. It is also the case that specific aspects of the Northern Soul scene imposed necessary differences. Platform-soled shoes and boots were a mainstream fashion in the early 70s, but they were wholly impractical for dancing and so were shunned by

*Forgotten fashions: The author in a blue 'L for Leather' pin-tuck leather jacket and a sheepskin coat (complete with Manchester United lapel badge). Both shots are from the late 1970s, but the leather jacket dates back to 1976, and I bought my first sheepskin when I started work in 1971. Under the leather jacket, I'm wearing a cap-sleeve T-shirt, and under the sheepskin, a skinny-rib jumper. These were very popular items at different stages of the 70s, which seem to have largely vanished from reinvented conceptions of 'Northern Soul fashion'.*

Northern Soul fans in favour of old-fashioned leather-soled brogues and the like. And whereas you'd be unlikely to get past the door of a regular club without jacket, collar and tie, the sweltering heat of Northern Soul all-nighter made the coloured cotton singlet acceptable attire.

What seems to have happened is that, when Northern Soul went over ground and press and video cameras made their way into Wigan Casino, that had the effect of preserving the scene in aspic: this was what Northern Soul people wore (and Wigan Casino was the place they wore it). The myth was established and there was the evidence to prove it. All of the subtlety, variation and history were lost.

It is, of course, an aspect of the way we live, that ideas become simplified and condensed into some easy-to-consume form – some kind of shorthand

– and we thus read the world through a succession of myths. Or, put another way, we read what is around us through an endless stream of media-fed over-simplifications and misunderstandings. It is also the case that among human societies of all kinds, the semiotic messages given off by clothes are subtle and read with great sensitivity by both the wearer and viewer (except in the case of those who don't care what they look like, but even then, 'not caring' is often a quite carefully studied act). Thus, when someone, now, looks at an old photograph of a roomful of 1970s Northern Soul kids and sees a more or less similar hotchpotch of fashions, they overlook the ways those people would have seen each other at the time or how those individuals felt when they chose and donned those clothes. At the time, some of those people

*The author in his sheepskin jacket.*

would have looked smart, cool, and well turned-out, and others would not; some would have been on trend, others would not. The subtleties of those perceptions are lost to those whose view is not informed by how things were at that time, in that place and among those people.

What is informative and encouraging is that, at contemporary Northern Soul events, people wear a variety of clothes. The baggies-and-bowling shirt look does occur, as does the badge-plastered vest, but so do the rolled-up Levis,

Doc Martens and Tonic suits of an earlier era. And some people just wear what would wear anyway, whether they were at a Northern Soul event or not. It was ever thus. Even in 1975, what many people wore to Northern Soul clubs, they also wore to the pub, to the football and to work.

There exists footage of fans going to a Leeds United versus Manchester United match in 1975 (I was probably at that one). It can be found, at the time of writing, on YouTube, set to a backcloth of 'Where Have All the Boot Boys Gone' by Slaughter and the Dogs.[33] It shows thousands of fans getting off trains and coaches, walking to the ground and gathering by the turnstiles.

They are nearly all young males, reflecting the nature of football fan-ship at that time. Almost everyone in shot is wearing baggies, collar-length hair and a pattern-fronted acrylic jumper or floppy-collared T-shirt. In short, everyone is wearing the 'Northern Soul look'. That is probably 50,000 or so people, just in Leeds, just near the football ground and just on that afternoon. Played out over the whole country, that would be hundreds of thousands of people, maybe a million plus, all wearing that look or something very similar, all when Northern Soul was still, relatively speaking, a minority interest. It had gone over ground to an extent, but it was of far less significance in popular culture than, say, Queen, David Bowie and Rod Stewart. The top disco sounds at the time were the likes of 'The Hustle' by Van McCoy, 'I Can't Give You Anything (But My Love)' by the Stylistics and 'That's the Way I Like It' by K C and the Sunshine band – not Northern Soul. The point is clear: this was not a specific Northern Soul fashion; it was the mode of the moment in general for working-class and lower-middle-class male teenagers and young men.

Looking at old photos of pop acts of the time – the Bay City Rollers and David Essex, for example – you see people wearing what looks like the Northern Soul look, when, of course, these acts had nothing to do with Northern Soul. With the exception of the odd tweak – like the badges, which not everyone wore, anyway – the mythologised Northern Soul uniform isn't so much the 'Northern Soul look' as the 'mid-70s teenager look', and that came and went from the scene along with many other styles.

---

[33] Slaughter and the Dogs. 1977 Where Have All the Boot Boys Gone (music and video) [online] Available https://www.youtube.com/watch?v=dILXRY8JiKg [online] [Accessed 19 April 2017]

## You had to have sports bag…?

No, you didn't.

The image of the Northern Soul boy/girl carrying an Adidas bag or other sports bag, usually plastered with badges referencing all of the famous clubs, is one of the most familiar Northern Soul stereotypes.

I have been going to Soul clubs on and off for most of my life, and I went to most of the major clubs in Northern Soul's 1970s heyday, and in all that time, I never owned such a bag, nor did any of my friends, and to the best of my recollection, I never saw any of the people I knew peripherally with one either.

Presumably, they contained a change of clothes; something that might be welcome in the morning after a long, sweaty all-nighter. So it is logical to think that, even from way back in the early days of the all-nighters, taking a bag would have been popular with a fastidious minority. But for most of us, going home in precisely what we had gone out in was the norm. Possibly this meant we stunk like polecats on the way back, but, if this were the case, no-one gave it a second thought, and the matter would be resolved with a bath on getting home.

What seems to have happened is that taking a bag, especially a bag covered with badges, is one of the things that became more popular when the scene went over ground. The bag becomes not only a practical thing, but a visible statement of identity. Even so, looking at photographs from the era of people queuing outside of all-nighters, only perhaps one in ten has a bag. Moreover, there is another attitude on the scene, as there always was, which does not feel the need for such public statements of identity. For those who take this position, the idea of actively eschewing what might be seen as immoderate public statements would be more valued. From this perspective, the bag's role as a practical necessity was dubious and a cover for its real function as an unnecessary and rather gauche flag of allegiance. It would therefore be regarded by this group within the Northern Soul fraternity as uncool, perhaps bandwagon-jumping or mindlessly following the herd, and possibly 'divvish' behaviour.

So, in short: some took bags, but most did not, and not having a bag was far from Northern Soul social suicide.

## Everyone went round plastered in Northern Soul badges, didn't they?

One of the enduring myths, perpetuated in various media, is that we all went around with our singlets, bowling shirts or baggy trousers covered in sewn-on patches, which celebrated the name of every Northern Soul club we could think of and/or remonstrated with anyone who cared to look to 'keep the faith'.

It isn't true.

Wigan Casino was arguably the home of Northern Soul hype and the place where, if you were going to see people plastered in badges, you would see them, but you don't: Wigan is one of the few Northern Soul haunts that was filmed and extensively photographed, and in none of those images will you see large numbers of people bedecked in badges. Some have one or two; only a small number have many.

In clubs away from and before Wigan Casino, such a sight would be even rarer. Fashions[34] in the earlier clubs, for a time at least, had their origins in the Mod scene and included such things as the Tonic suit, on which badges would be incongruous; though, the barathea blazer was briefly popular, worn with Tonic pants or faded jeans, and a single badge on the breast pocket was acceptable. A black Harrington or Levi or Wrangler denim jacket might just get the same treatment. However, it was more likely to be a Lancashire or Yorkshire rose than one proclaiming the name of a club.

It also needs to be borne in mind that even when Wigan Casino was up and running, it was not the only show in town, and what was typical at Wigan was not necessarily typical elsewhere. The publicity that Wigan Casino drew to itself has made the club synonymous with Northern Soul in the popular imagination. However, many did not take to the hype and hysteria that the

---

[34] See separate section on this: 'Everyone wore baggy pants and a bowling shirt, didn't they?'

*Inside Wigan Casino, circa 1976/7. Photo credit: Gillian Scott Moore.*

place engendered, and attitudes that existed before Wigan persisted: attitudes that valued cool and style and not doing as you were told or following trends unquestioningly. Moreover, many who came to the scene during Wigan's putative pre-eminence did not necessarily conform to the stereotypes that have come down to us, and many who tried Wigan found themselves happier at Blackpool Mecca, the Talk of the North (Cleethorpes) all-nighter and other alternative venues. And some who went to these places endeavoured to distance themselves from Wigan Casino and its excesses. Indeed, many who went to Wigan still observed concepts of cool in their clothing choices and avoided the more demonstrative gestures.

Moreover, for a good proportion of Northern Soul's heyday, the term 'Northern Soul' did not exist or had not gained common currency, so badges with those words did not exist. We saw ourselves just as followers of Soul music, and whereas we might be dancing to 100mph Soul stompers on a Saturday night, we might be chilling to Soul ballads on a Sunday afternoon.

In short: some wore the odd badge, very few wore lots, most wore none, and many regarded the wearing of them as gauche. You were as likely to see a T-shirt with an Adidas or a Fred Perry logo, or a bowling shirt carrying an ad for some bogus American university or diner or car repair shop, as a top covered in Northern Soul patches. And more common than all of those was just unadorned clothing, drawn from the fashions of the day.

## Wigan Casino was the birth place of Northern Soul, wasn't it?

If you, dear reader, are someone who has spent some time on the Northern Soul scene, or even if you are new to it and have read this far through this book, you will know that this is not true. It is, however, a persistent myth. I mentioned in the opening part of the book the fact that a Telegraph journalist had glibly written that, with the opening of the doors of Wigan Casino in 1973, Northern Soul was born. That is of course very slack journalism and wholly inaccurate, but it is a view shared by many. Others see 'Wigan Casino' and 'Northern Soul' as synonymous, interchangeable. For some, Wigan Casino wasn't only the birthplace of Northern Soul, it was the place where Northern Soul happened, and the only place where Northern Soul happened.

*Wigan Casino, circa 1976/7. Photo credit: Gillian Scott Moore*

Without wishing to write a history of Northern Soul – many others have done that admirably elsewhere – we can at least summarise by saying that Wigan Casino was only one of many Northern Soul clubs and it was not the first or the best. When it opened in the autumn of 1973, a Northern Soul scene, or something rather like it, had been around for most of a decade: since the Mod clubs of the early to mid 60s had made black American dance music – RnB and early Rhythm and Soul – a central part of their playlists. When Wigan Casino opened, it delivered a format that had taken shape in earlier clubs, like The Twisted Wheel, The Torch, The Catacombs and Va-Va. It even featured some of the same DJs, and much of what it played had already been popularised at those other venues.

What we can say also about Wigan Casino, however, is that it became the biggest and most visible of the Northern Soul clubs, due to more creative and aggressive marketing by its proprietors than had been seen at other clubs. That, however, came at a price and, while the myth of Wigan Casino being the birth place of Northern Soul stands no scrutiny whatsoever, it could be reasonably argued that it was the death place of Northern Soul.

I say this for two reasons. Firstly, in the most basic terms, Wigan Casino happened to be the one major club still going when Northern Soul fizzled out, in the way most youth cults do: those attending grow up and move away from the scene. Like a game of pass-the-parcel, Wigan Casino just happened to be holding the package when the music stopped – or when some vital aspect of it stopped. But there is a second aspect, one in which Wigan Casino can be seen as creating a format for Northern Soul in which its demise was assured. I say this whilst acknowledging that Northern Soul carried on and still exists in various forms – I say much more on this below – but the way the original Northern Soul scene created and maintained itself ended at Wigan Casino.

As stated elsewhere in this book, Northern Soul, as it emerged, played both old records and new ones that had the right sound. In the 60s, all the records were new. In the early 70s, you would hear new recordings like 'This is the House Where Love Died' by First Choice, 'K-Jee' by The Nite-Liters and 'Put it Where You Want It' by The Crusaders, next to 60s tracks like 'I've Got Something Good' by Sam and Kitty and 'Love You Baby' by Eddie Parker. Indeed, Wigan Casino continued with this proven format at first: I distinctly recall 'The Zoo' by The Commodores, 'The Joker' by the Watts 103rd Street Rhythm Band, 'Hung Up on Your Love' by the Montclairs and many more 'modern' sounds at Wigan Casino. However, there then came the famous Northern Soul schism: Blackpool Mecca followed contemporary danceable Soul music; Wigan Casino followed the 60s beat, whether the music was Soul or not. Thus, ultimately, Wigan ended up playing Northern Soul tracks that had been around the block many, many times, along with a large amount of white pop music, and it is hard to say that a club is perpetuating a Soul scene when much of its output isn't Soul.

I mention elsewhere that Midlands-based Soul fan who by 1975 saw Wigan Casino as a 'circus' and decided he could no longer justify travelling there to hear the kind of music it was playing. Many others had the same experience – myself included. I can remember watching the dancefloor go crazy to 'Footsee', 'Goodbye Nothing to Say', 'Hawaii 5-0', 'Papa Ooh Mow Mow' and others of that ilk, and getting a distinct sense of something some way beyond disquiet. 'Footsee' sounded to me very much like the theme music to a kids' tv show called 'Banana Splits', which I'd seen in my early teens and which involved actors dressed in furry animal suits. Given that TV and film themes, down to and including the 'Joe 90 Theme' (the theme music to a 1960s children's puppet show), were by now considered 'Soul music' good enough for a Wigan Casino audience, it would not have been surprising to hear that, though as far as I know it was never played.

It wasn't just that it was bad music – many of us felt patronised. I had the clear sense of an attitude that said, 'you fools will dance to anything'. That may be just projection, but that's how it felt. I was also dismayed that so many thought this music was great, when I didn't. There were other strange things happening too: the type of dancing that I'd got used to involved one foot stepping back and forth, with the other doing a James Brown-esque toe-and-heel slide across the floor, then switching feet and sliding back. At Wigan I'd started to notice this odd sort of 'kicking-out' action. Only much later did I hear that a Footsee was a children's toy, and the record of the same name was from the advert for it. The toy was a sort of ankle hoola-hoop, with a ball attached to it by a length of string. The thing was to be played with by kicking out and spinning it around your ankle. I then learned there was such a thing as 'doing' The Footsee – dancing like you were wearing one of these toys. Evidently, this kicking-out dance I'd seen at Wigan was people 'doing The Footsee' – emulating playing with this toy.

At Northern Soul clubs that had Ian Levine, Colin Curtis and quite a few notable others behind the decks, you had a clear sense of a fellow Soul fan taking to the stage and the music being a shared passion. But at Wigan Casino, as its output become ever more dubious, there came a sense of hierarchy, of someone doling out any old crap from above, in the belief that because of the naivety of the listenership and because this was Wigan Casino, they could get away with it. Unfortunately, it was a view that was proved correct. However, many saw through it and moved on to other clubs. As for me,

I was 21 in the summer of 1976, when I went to Wigan Casino for the last time. I was well past being subjected to the kind of condescension this music represented or being cajoled into playing children's games.

To exacerbate the situation, this was happening at the time when Northern Soul had gone over ground, with Wigan Casino as the flagship club. So, just at the moment when the largest number of people were getting into Northern Soul for the first time, Soul music itself was on the retreat in the most influential 'Northern Soul' club, and we had the extraordinary situation that the club defining itself as the 'Heart of Soul' was driving away lovers of Soul music, who couldn't bear the playlists any longer, whilst drawing in a new and large crowd and educating their tastes to a style of Soul that wasn't actually Soul at all. The upshot being a generation of Northern Soul fans who were reared to a significant degree on non-Soul passed off as Northern Soul.

The derogatory term 'divs' was often used for those who mindlessly followed what were seen as the more tasteless fads. It's a term that sounds uncomfortable at this distance, when everyone who went to those clubs in those days – cool or otherwise – is now of venerable age, or dead, and worthy of a degree of respect. Plus, we were all divs once, if div refers to that period when you have just arrived on the scene and are still that gangly youth who hasn't yet quite 'got it'. However, what happened at Wigan was that there was a huge number of newbies all at once, many of whom never really got it and didn't stick around for long and latched onto the scene's superficial images and bad but foregrounded records, and believe that skewed perception of the Soul scene was the real and only one. Thus, records by a Lancastrian club-circuit band and tunes from TV shows and those from adverts for toys are Soul records for large numbers of people.

If this seems a little far-fetched, social media can be instructive. There are many Northern Soul groups on Facebook, but the one named just 'Northern Soul' is the most populous and the site of some extraordinary exchanges, which reveal the influence of that era of the Northern Soul scene on attitudes that persist to this day. There are other more specialised Northern Soul groups, often dedicated to one club, and with far fewer members. As illustration, the Northern Soul group has around 28,000 members, at the time of writing, whereas The Twisted Wheel Club group has about 1,600, and The Blackpool Mecca Appreciation Society has just over 2,000. Probably because of its size and the specificity of its name, the Northern Soul group seems to attract people with the widest variety of views and levels of understanding of Northern Soul, from those who know the scene inside-out, to those with just a cursory knowledge, to those with no knowledge whatsoever but strongly held opinions. However, social media is a great leveller, and all can express their views, with whatever level of vehemence they choose, regardless of whether or not they know what they are talking about, and all from a position of relative anonymity and unaccountability. The myths, strange attitudes and viewpoints, and sometimes statements which are just plainly wrong, expressed within that group have been significant in prompting me to write this book. I need to be clear, however, that the large number of people on the site who know their stuff have often shouted the nonsense down. Indeed, it is sometimes what happens when these the exchanges take place that is most revealing. What follows is indicative.

In 2014 and through to 2015 the screening of the film *Northern Soul* (2014) produced a huge surge of interest in the scene and music, and this was naturally reflected in the Northern Soul group. This is where and when many of the posts by the rose-coloured-specs brigade, who deny there was any drug use or violence on the scene, appeared. There was also a spate of people discussing their favourite Northern Soul sounds and posting them online for others to hear and 'like'. Over and over again, the tracks that came up were 'The Night' by Frankie Valli and the Four Seasons, 'Under my Thumb' by Wayne Gibson, 'What' by Judy Street, 'There's a Ghost in My House' by R. Dean Taylor, 'Nine Times Out of Ten' by Muriel Day, 'Footsee' by Wigan's Chosen Few, and 'Skiing in the Snow' by Wigan's Ovation. The things all these records have in common are, firstly, that they are among Wigan Casino's most popular tracks and, secondly, that none of them is a Soul record; in fact, most of them aren't even American. Muriel Day is Irish, Wigan's Ovation and Wayne Gibson are British, and Footsee is a British reworking of a Canadian record.

The other two top tracks were Frank Wilson's 'Do I Love You' and Al Wilson's 'The Snake', which are, of course, Soul records. With the above, these would complete what for many would be Wigan Casino's 'greatest hits'. For such a large proportion of a Soul club's most memorable songs not to be Soul songs at all is really quite something.

I have made it clear throughout this book that Northern Soul was never only about black music; there always was some white pop/RnB too, but that tended to be a small intervention into what was, overall, a black music scene. What these records demonstrate, in the high esteem accorded to them and in the large numbers who hold them in that high esteem, is that most of the music most loved by the largest number in Wigan Casino's moment in the sun was not Soul at all – it was 60s pop. Clearly, other records – actual Soul records, as well as further pop records – were loved too, but they play second-fiddle to this handful of monster tracks. And this has created a legacy of people who believe they have a taste for Soul but in fact have a taste for something else. As an experiment, when this was going on, when I saw a flurry of activity on the Northern Soul group around these tracks, I posted 'Love Man' by Otis Redding, to see what reaction it would get. I chose that track in particular because, for me, it is one of the best examples of a place where a real Soul voice – one of the best Soul voices of the lot, arguably – and a fantastic danceable backing track come together. But, whilst Muriel Day, Wayne Gibson and the rest received hundreds of 'likes', Otis received none. It's hard to escape the thought that there is a constituency out there that believes it likes Soul, but in truth finds it a bit heavy going.

Looking at postings on the Northern Soul group at the time of writing, Muriel Day's 'Nine Times Out of Ten' is on there again. With the buzz created by the Northern Soul movies having died down, the group is less busy, the song has been seen by fewer people and it has far fewer 'likes': just 60, compared to 200-300 back when things were livelier. Nearby is Linda Jones' stunning 'My Heart Needs a Break' – it has 3 'likes'.

I am aware that what I am writing here will offend many, but that does not make it untrue. Nevertheless, I feel a need to make clear what I am saying and what I am not saying. I am not saying Wigan Casino was a lousy club: I had some great times there, as did many others. I am not saying all the music there was bad: there was some great music played there, as well as some rubbish. I am not saying all the DJs were naff: many of the DJs were great and were responsible for discovering some of Northern Soul's finest sounds. I am not saying DJs in other clubs didn't spin the odd dodgy white pop record; they did – it's just that they were more selective and didn't play as many or plumb the depths that Wigan did.[35] What I am saying is that at some point someone took their eye off the ball and there was a drift into some shockingly bad music. It is perfectly possible to put together a three-hour plus playlist of music heard at Wigan Casino and/or performed by acts that carry its name, and not hear one black singer. You don't believe me? Check out this list of Wigan Casino-related records which are by white artistes, or sound very much like they are by white artistes, or are instrumentals whose connection to Soul is pretty tenuous:

Hold On – The Generation
Ten to One – Lou Roberts and the Marks
You Fooled Me – Lou Roberts and the Marks

---

[35] In the early pages of this book I write about some of the white and other non-soul music played way back at the Twisted Wheel. However, I think it is fair to say that The Wheel didn't play such a large proportion of such dubious records. Plus, The Wheel also has a certain get-out clause in this, in that it was established long before 'Northern Soul' was defined as an entity and even before the term 'Soul' had gained much currency. It therefore never promised a diet of solely Soul music. Wigan Casino, on the other hand, defined itself as a 'Soul Club' on its badges, flyers and membership cards.

Born a Loser – Don Ray
Goodbye Nothing to Say – Nosmo King/Javells
Footsee – Wigan's Chosen Few
Skiing in the Snow – Wigan's Ovation
That's Not Love – Holly St James
Don't Turn Me Loose – The Newbeats
Joe 90 Theme – The Ron Grainger Orchestra
Hawaii Five-0 – The Ventures
Glad All Over (Instrumental) – The Leon Young Strings
Panic – Reperata and the Delores
It's Waiting There for You – Reperata and the Delrons
Love's the Only Answer – Kelly Garrett
Village of Tears – Ben Zine
Elusive – Babe Ruth
Too Many People – Bobby Goldsboro
It's Too Late – Bobby Goldsboro
When We Get There – Paul Anka
Can't Help Loving You – Paul Anka
Rat Race – The Righteous Brothers Orchestra
If You Loved Me – Peggy March
I Walked Away – Bobby Paris
Night Owl – Bobby Paris
Per-so-nal-ly – Bobby Paris
Per-so-nal-ly – Wigan's Ovation
Breakaway – Toni Basil
I'm on My Way – Dean Parrish
I Need You – Shane Martin
By Yourself – Jay D Martin
Wall to Wall Heartaches – Bobby Jason
Condition Red – The Baltimore and Ohio Marching Band
Man Without a Woman – Michael and Raymond
Lost Summer Love – Lorraine Silver
Stop and You Will Become Aware – Helen Shapiro
Out of My Mind – Rain
What – Judy Street
The Larue – Lada Edmund Jnr.
There's Ghost in My House – R. Dean Taylor
Theme from Police Story – Pat Williams Orchestra
The Wigan Joker – The Allnight Band
Interplay – Derek and Ray
The Night – Frankie Valli and the Four Seasons
I'm Gonna Change – Frankie Valli and the Four Seasons
Trick Me, Treat Me – Cobblestone

I'll Do Anything – Tony Blackburn
What's It Gonna Be – Dusty Springfield
What's It Gonna be – Susan Barrett
Keeps on Burning – The Burning Bush
Nine Time Out of Ten – Muriel Day
Too Much of a Good Thing - Karen Young
You've Got Your Mind On Other Things – Beverley Ann
He's Coming Home – Beverley Ann
Superlove – David and the Giants
Superlove – Wigan's Ovation
Ten Miles High – David and the Giants
Daylight Saving Time – Keith
My Heart's Symphony – Gary Lewis and the Playboys
How Can I Forget – Joey Dee and the Starlighters
And Suddenly – The Cherry People
Under My Thumb – Wayne Gibson
The Joker Went Wild – Brian Hyland
We know We're in Love – Lesley Gore
Up and Over – Jay Traynor
You Got Me Where You Want Me – Larry Santos
Salt and Pepper – The Esko Affair
Music with Soul – The Pallbearers
Playing Hide and Seek – Eddie Regan
Woman, Lover Thief – Stemmons Express
Hang On – Wall of Sound
He'll Never Love You Like I Do – Charlie Gracie
We Go Together – August and Deneen
Like Adam and Eve – The Reflections
Don't Pity Me – Joanie Summers
Don't Pity Me – Sue Lynn
I'm Getting' on Life – Wombat
You Can't Mean It – Chapter Five
Name It You Got It – Mickey Moonshine
I'll Hold You – Frankie and Johnny
I Wanna Know – John E Paul

I'm not saying these are all bad and/or unsoulful records – some are great records and some are very soulful – and I'm not saying that many didn't also get played in other clubs or that some didn't start out at other venues. However, a substantial proportion are primarily or solely Wigan sounds, and those who went to Wigan Casino in the mid to late-70s will know that what they see here is a sizeable part of what they heard, and such a concentration of white pop records in a club that was supposed to be the focal point of a specialist Soul scene is something that can't be ignored. Plus, some of these tracks really are truly dreadful and the connection of many to Soul music is way beyond dubious.

I should say that I can't be absolutely certain that there are no black musicians involved here, and I apologise without reservation if I have misrepresented anyone in compiling this list. Many of these acts are obscure and details about some of them are hard to find. However, most are clearly identified and there are still further such tracks I could have added, and many reading this will know of yet more that could be added to this list.

This isn't about being a Soul 'purist' or insisting on a black-only playlist. Northern Soul always played some 'blue-eyed Soul'. 'Determination' by white, Spanish-Italian New Yorker, Dean Parrish, is one of Northern Soul's most powerful and enduring tracks, and black singers are not immune from producing duff records. So, I am very much not saying all white records were poor or out of place. Records like 'The Larue' by Lada Edmund Junior and 'Love's the Only Answer' by Kelly Garrett are examples of stonking white Northern Soul records, played all over, where there is a dynamic vocal performance over a backing track not out of place in a Soul environment, and where everything comes together so well that the question of whether the singer was black or white would be unlikely to cross anyone's mind. And I would further argue that these records would not have been improved upon much, even if Etta James or Nancy Wilson had been behind the microphone. I could even go further: I think Paul Anka's version of 'Can't Help Loving You' is better than Jimmy Breedlove's, though the reason I think this is that it is very much a producer's record, and the Anka version is a beefier, faster, better production. For the same reason, The Four Season's 'I'm Gonna Change' beats the Velours' version, in my opinion. On the other hand, I have no idea what records like 'Born a Loser' by Don Ray, 'And Suddenly' by the Cherry People, 'I'll Do Anything' by Tony Blackburn[36] and many others on this list are doing in a Soul club. In short, the issue is one of quality, quantity and whether a thing really, audibly fits into the Soul paradigm – not skin colour.

This skewing of the concept of Soul music has twisted what Northern Soul means for a lay audience and for some latecomers to the scene. This has produced some extraordinary moments on social media. Presumably prompted by the playing on the Northern Soul scene of Bobby Goldsboro's 'It's Too Late' and 'Too Many People', which already stretched the notion of 'Soul

---

[36] I should add in defence of Tony Blackburn, that he has been a great friend to Soul music as a DJ, but DJ-ing is his thing, and having heard him interviewed on this matter, he is as dismissive of this record as anyone else with properly functioning ears.

music' beyond breaking point, someone posted Goldsboro's sickly, big-hit ballad 'Honey' on the Northern Soul group on Facebook. You might reasonably expect that to have been met with horror and dismay, but it got scores of 'likes'. Someone else posted 'Move Over Darling' by Doris Day. When asked what the hell he was playing at, the poster accused the complainer of being new to Northern Soul and not really knowing what he was talking about.

Slightly less embarrassingly, some people post 1970s pop-Soul records on the Northern Soul group, often to rapturous applause in the form of 'likes' and effusive comments from a largish number of people; records such as 'You Can Do Magic' by Limmie and Family Cookin', or 'Sad Sweet Dreamer' by Sweet Sensation, or the Drifters' mum-and-dad-oriented mid-70s ballads, or Billy Ocean's Motown/Northern Soul clone records, or Hot Chocolate's output. Rows then break out between those who insist this music has nothing to do with Northern Soul and those who insist that it does and that no-one has a right to dictate what Northern Soul is. What I can say, unequivocally, is that I never heard these records or their ilk in any Northern Soul club I went to. That was the sort of music that was played at youth clubs and ordinary, non-Northern Soul discos. It was the kind of music we went to Northern Soul clubs to avoid. I can't imagine any Northern Soul DJ, back in the day, thinking for one moment of spinning records like these. Some, I think, might have feared for their safety had they done so. It seems the concept of Northern Soul has, for some, drifted to 'anything I heard in my teenage years'.

The position outlined above, which argues that no-one has the right to say what is and what isn't a Northern Soul record, sounds fair and reasonable at first glance, but if you follow that through to its natural conclusion, you end up having to agree that 'Remember You're a Womble' and Rolf Harris's 'Two Little Boys' are Northern Soul records, if someone says they are. If that sounds absurd, consider the following: a mid-60s single called 'The Joker' by Norman Wisdom (described in Wikipedia as 'English actor, comedian, and singer-songwriter best known for a series of comedy films produced between 1953 and 1966 featuring his hapless onscreen character Norman Pitkin')[37], has been proffered for sale as 'Northern Soul' on an internet auction site. I don't know if that version ever got played at Wigan Casino – I doubt it, but the fact that someone could make that association speaks volumes. And, whatever the case, there is another version, by Shawn Elliott, which is not dissimilar and which was played there.

---

[37] Wikipedia [online] Norman Wisdom Available: https://en.wikipedia.org/wiki/Norman_Wisdom [Accessed 3 June 2016] – I wouldn't normally use Wikipedia as a source, but Norman Wisdom is so well known that it hardly matters in this case.

At that point, it is hard not to say that the bottom of the barrel has been well and truly scraped. Add to that songs like the cluster of trashy cash-in records that had the word 'Wigan' attached to them, and we can see that a direction has been followed that has an inevitable and awful end. If records excruciatingly dreadful as these can be passed off as 'Northern Soul', then Northern Soul really has died.

Of course, anyone is entitled to like anything they want to, and if someone has a taste for 1960s pop, including records by Norman Wisdom, they're absolutely entitled to it. I like some 60s pop – the Kinks, the Small Faces and even some Beach Boys tracks – but that doesn't make these Soul acts. So, what I am objecting to here is not the fact that some people like Muriel Day and the rest, but that they form a large body of opinion that believes this is 'Soul' and in their weight of numbers skew perceptions both of what (Northern) Soul music is and what the scene was like.

Whilst the media were carrying their video cameras into Wigan Casino in the mid/late-70s and making what few bits of footage there are of the Northern Soul scene and thereby inadvertently creating many of Northern Soul's myths, I and many others were at Talk of the North in Cleethorpes, The Ritz all-dayer in Manchester and Blackpool Mecca, listening to brilliant black American dance music that we regarded as Northern Soul. The focus on Wigan Casino and its strange playlists and the disregarding of what was going on elsewhere on the scene distorted perceptions of what Northern Soul was and continues to do so.

## It was all about 60s music, wasn't it; none of that 70s music or that disco stuff?

Nope, that's not true either, but it is another widely disseminated myth. Many want to put space between 'Northern Soul' and 'disco' music, and you can easily see why. The story would go something like this: Northern Soul, in its heyday at least, offered aficionados a euphoric mixture of the best music, the coolest fashions and the dark appeal operating on the margins of society and legality. Disco, on the other hand, had embarrassingly bad music, and to be associated with that scene was, by inference, to be someone who hadn't got a clue about music, fashion or style and did not hang out with the right crowd. Such a story would, however, be a distortion and a massive oversimplification.

Firstly, it isn't true that 'disco' only had lousy music and bad fashions (or, indeed, that everything played at Northern Soul clubs was above suspicion; and it is hardly the case that all of its devotees had great dress sense). The music played in ordinary clubs was always questionable because it was so varied and could include anything that could be danced to, from Suzi Quatro to Gilbert O'Sullivan to Cliff Richard. But there is a clear emergence of a 'disco' scene in the early 70s that focused mostly on black music and had a degree of credibility, until it got hijacked by Boney M, Leo Sayer, Rick Dees and His Cast of Idiots and the rest, and became a joke. Many American acts aired their new 'disco' tunes on Soul Train, which was at the cutting edge of American black music and fashion. Those fashions, like those at Northern Soul clubs, may look laughable now, as old fashions tend to, but at the time they were radical, daring and edgy. The acts featured on Soul Train in the disco era read like a 'who's who' of Soul music and almost all of them produced music you could dance to: Jerry Butler, The Whispers, Mandrill, Eddie Kendricks, Ecstasy, Passion and Pain, Marvin Gaye, Gladys Knight and the Pips, to name a few. Regular discos and Northern Soul clubs played music by acts who were featured on Soul Train, and although the disco scene and the Northern Soul scene may have picked different part of these acts' repertoires, that was not always the case and sometimes they played the actual same records. See below.

Secondly, Northern Soul was disco – it was just a different form of disco from the one most people mean when they use the term. A 'disco' is just a 'discotheque', and a 'discotheque' is a dance hall where they play records rather than live music. Live acts did appear at Northern Soul events, but they were rare, and the scene relied almost entirely on 7" discs. The words 'disco' and 'discotheque' crop up repeatedly in relation to Northern Soul. One of Northern Soul's earliest and most enduring tracks is 'At the Discotheque' by Chubby Checker. In 1966 the UK Capitol label released a series of records which became Northern Soul favourites under the heading 'Discotheque '66 Series'. The flurry of Northern Soul 7" rereleases put out on the Pye label in the mid-70s had 'Disco Demand' emblazoned across the middle – in much bigger and bolder letters than the song title, the artistes' name or even Pye's logo. In 1974, Pye released a Northern Soul compilation called 'Disco Demand's Solid Soul Sensations – 16 Previously Unreleased Northern Soul Sounds'. In 1975, they released another, called 'Great Disco Demands'. Both had a little logo on the sleeve featuring a picture of a cowboy and the words 'Disco Kid'. Also in 1975 and still under the auspices of Pye Records, but this time on the Stax label, another compilation appeared, called 'Stax Northern Disco Sounds'. Clearly, at this stage at least, there was no embarrassment about calling a Northern Soul club a 'disco'; indeed, Pye plainly saw it as a selling point. And, whereas Northern Soul fans would want to distinguish their discos from the 'divvy' discos, the cringing embarrassment created by acts like Liquid Gold, the Bee Gees and The Nolans, with their dancing, romancing and chancing, had yet to occur. A good deal of 'disco' music at that time was respected, even if it was deemed unsuitable for Northern Soul clubs. Songs like The Intruders' 'I'll Always Love My Mama', Eddie Kendricks' 'Keep on Truckin'' and Don Downing's 'Dreamworld' are the kinds of tracks that didn't quite have the right pace for a Northern Soul club, but might otherwise be regarded as pretty good stuff, and some collectors would have bought both this type of music and Northern Soul, whilst being cognisant of the difference. Some acts had hits with one lot of records in the Northern Soul clubs whilst having hits with others in the regular discos and pop charts. Whilst the world at large was listening to the O'Jays' 'Backstabbers', '992 Arguments' and 'Love Train', Northern Soul fans were dancing to 'Deeper (In Love With You)', 'Looky Looky (At Me Girl)' and 'Lipstick Traces', all of which were unknown to a lay audience. The distinction here lies in the style, the era and accessibility; the Northern Soul records all being 1960s recordings and hard to find, whilst the others were on general release.

Rarity mattered, but sometimes the margins were small: whilst folk at the regular disco were getting down to First Choice's 'Armed and Extremely Dangerous' in 1973, Northern Soul fiends at The Torch were dancing to 'This is the House Where Love Died' by the same trio. The latter had only been released in the previous year and, indeed, had been played on the scene since it was new. However, it had the kudos of being only available on import, so only those who used the few specialist record shops that stocked such things or were acquainted with the right mail-order import suppliers would have access to it, and then only if those stockists actually had copies to sell. It was also probably a better record – although the two are similar in style, 'Armed and Extremely Dangerous' had a rather corny, Dragnet-style police voiceover at the beginning.

The margins get even smaller: 'Put it Where You Want It' by The Crusaders, 'K-Jee' by the Nite-Liters, and 'My Man a Sweet Man' by Millie Jackson are all records that were spun at The Torch whilst they were on general release and available for any DJ to play at any kind of disco. I distinctly remember dancing to the Millie Jackson track at Manchester Beer Keller – very much not a Northern Soul venue – in 1972. It also made the lower reaches of the pop charts in the same year.

'Scrub-Board' by The Trammps is even more anomalous. It was an instrumental and a B-side (of 'Sixty Minute Man'), played and well received at The Torch in 1972-3. A vocal version – 'Hold Back the Night', came out in 1975, was a big hit in the regular discos as well as in the pop charts, but was largely ignored by Northern Soul clubs. This may have been because of its general popularity, but it was also often case on the Northern Soul scene that a new release would be played until the regular discos and general pubic caught wind of it, then it would be dropped. What aided this practice was the fact that Soul records would generally be released in the US quite some time before they came out in the UK, and sometimes they didn't come out in the UK at all, so Northern Soul jocks would pick up on a new song as an import and spin it before those who had no access to imports would even know of its existence. Absolute rarity mattered, but here was a kind of conditional rarity and temporary exclusiveness. But to the best of my recollection, 'Hold Back the Night' was never even accorded this privilege, and what seems to have happened is that between 1972 and 1975, the concept of 'Northern Soul' had taken root and that could no longer tolerate the skip-along Philly sound of 'Hold Back the Night'. But, whatever the case, it is fact that 'Scrub-Board' was played in Northern Soul discos and the almost identical 'Hold Back the Night' was played in 'disco' discos (and it is also possible that some regular disco jocks played 'Scrub-Board' and some Northern Soul DJs gave 'Hold Back the Night' the odd airing, but I never heard it played), so it is clear that there was an overlap between the two scenes and in the style of what was played, and not the complete separation that some would suggest.

Since first drafting the above, I have been contacted by a friend who recalls hearing 'Hold Back the Night', played as a 'prelease' in Northern Soul clubs 1975 and then for a few months afterwards, up to the point when it went over ground, made it into the regular discos and became a chart hit. But the points made still stand: 'Scrub Board' was a monster track at the Torch, 'Hold Back the Night' achieved some brief Northern Soul popularity but was then dropped once the mainstream got hold of it, and there was a fluid, reciprocal relationship between the Northern Soul scene and a number of notionally 'disco' records.

Thirdly and most fundamentally, the term 'Northern Soul' didn't gain currency until about 1973/4 – and many years later in the States – so none of the artistes who made Northern Soul records had heard of Northern Soul when they did so. Thus, the dance music they made was for consumption in discotheques – discos – of any sort, anywhere. There is no separate category of 'Northern Soul' – the Northern Soul scene just separated off the music it liked from music made for discos in general.

There are two issues at work here, which are contrary to what some believe: firstly, the Northern Soul scene did play brand new music in the 70s and was not a 60s-only scene; secondly, the Northern Soul scene played music that was also played in regular discos. Among the 1970s releases that were played both at Northern Soul clubs and in regular discos, and in some cases charted, are 'I Love Music' by the O'Jays, 'Love Don't You Go Through No Changes on Me' by Sister Sledge, 'In the Bottle' by Gil Scott Heron, 'Love Machine' by the Miracles, 'Three Steps From True Love' by The Reflections (and Billy Davis's version), 'It Only Takes a Minute' and 'Heaven Must Be Missing an Angel' by Tavares, 'Do What You Feel' by the Rimshots, 'Don't Leave Me This Way' – Thelma Houston (and Harold Melvin and the Blue Notes' version), and 'The Flasher' by Mistura featuring Lloyd Michels. These records are well known to many who were into Soul and disco in the 70s, whether they had any involvement in Northern Soul or not. 'The Flasher' even made it onto Top of the Pops in 1976 (and was danced to by Ruby Flipper, unfortunately). It is also the case that Blackpool Mecca and clubs influenced by it – and sometimes hosted by the same DJs – played sounds as mainstream as Donna Summer and Chic, but by that stage it was fairly clear that the schism was becoming a reality and a scene that was no longer the Northern Soul scene was underway in these establishments. However, it remains true that there are a huge number of 1970s tracks that had no discernible audience in the mainstream and were only heard at venues regarded as part of the Northern Soul circuit.

Many of those who wish to expunge 70s music from the Northern Soul canon dismiss it as 'modern' sounding, and yet there are a large number of Northern Soul tracks from the 70s that sound like they were from the 70s and feature in that well known 'Northern Soul Top 500'. For some, there sometimes seems to be a kind of double-think at work, which says something like: 'if it isn't from the 60s it isn't Northern Soul – unless I like it'.

The following is a list (incomplete, and in addition to the above) of 1970s recordings that were played at Northern Soul clubs of various persuasions. Some will dismiss some of these as 'Mecca sounds' or 'modern Soul', but the experience of a clubber going to a variety of Northern Soul venues across the North and Midlands was one of hearing this music, as well as 60s stuff, under the heading of 'Northern Soul'. It suits some to imagine a complete black-and-white separation between 'Northern Soul', read as 'traditional 60s-sounding stuff, plus Wigan's diet of white 60s-beat pop', and 'Mecca/modern', often dismissed, wrongly in my view, as 'disco', 'funk' or 'jazz-funk'. Whereas Blackpool Mecca did end up playing music that might be filed under those headings, almost none of what I list below is funky or jazzy, and as for 'disco': as I have already set out above, there always was an overlap. These are still straightforward 4/4 beat, up-tempo and mid-tempo Soul records, without the jerky beat of funk or the protracted improvisations of jazz. Check out Funkadelic to hear the difference. Whereas the gap between Blackpool Mecca and Wigan Casino grew, in that early-to-mid-70s period in which Northern Soul still had some verve and creativity, there were overlaps and many styles of music were played. Also, Blackpool Mecca and Wigan Casino were not the only clubs. Venues with a broad, across-the-board ethic – like The Ritz all-dayer and the Cleethorpes all-nighter – played the new and the old without discrimination, as Northern Soul traditionally had. But then, so did Wigan Casino for its first few years. Even if Wigan did drift into playing some awful pop music, passed off as Soul, what was played, and when, depended on who was DJ-ing; and many (most?) of the tracks on this list of 1970s records will have been heard at some point at Wigan Casino:

Come on Train – Don Thomas
You've Come a Long Way Baby – The Flower Shoppe
Livin' in Love – Sheila Anthony
Exodus – Biddu Orchestra
You Touched Me – Judy Harris
I've Got the Need – 3 versions (at least): Chuck Jackson, The Moments, Spooky & Sue
Cashing In – The Voices of East Harlem
I Can See Him Loving You – The Anderson Brothers
It Really Hurts Me Girl – The Carstairs

Hung Up on Your Love – The Montclairs
You Better Keep Her – Marvin Holmes and Justice
Talkin' 'Bout Poor Folk – Lou Edwards and Today's People
Summer in the Parks – East Coast Connection
The Gig – Raw Soul
Love Factory – Eloise Laws
Are You Ready for This – The Brothers
Ella Weez – Leroy Hutson
Sweet Sweet Lady – The Moments
Lady Lady Lady – The Boogie Man Orchestra
Don't You Care Anymore – Jodi Mathis
Spring Rain - Silvetti
Seven Day Lover – James Fountain
Happy – Velvet Hammer
I Don't Know What Foot to Dance On – Kim Tolliver
You Made Me This Way – Ila Vann
Bet You If You Ask Around – Velvet
Bet You If You Check It Out – The Quadraphonics
The Soul of a Woman – Margo Thunder
The Ladies Choice – Boby Franklin
Lend a Hand – Bobby Hutton
The Devil Made Me Do It – The Natural Four
Cut Your Motor Off – Black Nasty
Find My Way – The Cameo Players (aka Cameo)
Game Players – Dooley Silverspoon
Can't Live This Way – Barnaby Bye
Dreaming a Dream – Crown Heights Affair
Foxy Lady – Crown Heights Affair
Send Him Back – The Pointer Sisters
Right On – Al de Lory and Mandango
Lord, What's Happening to Your People – Kenny Smith
I'm Your Pimp – The Skullsnaps
My Hang-Up is You – The Skullsnaps
If You and I Had Never Met – The Magic Night
What a Difference a Day Makes – Esther Phillips
Have Love Will Travel – Rosey Jones
Wrong Crowd – Prince George
That Girl is Rated X – Prince Johnny Robinson
Don't Depend On Me – Fantastic Johnny C
On the Real Side – Larry Saunders
Soon Everything is Gonna Be Alright –The Third Time Around
Whole Thing – Eighth Avenue Band
Turn the Beat Around – Vicky Sue Robinson

I'm Shaft (You Ain't Shaft) – R B Freeman
S.O.S. (All We Need is Time for Love) – Today's People
I've Got What You Need – Oscar Perry and the Love Generators
Let Me Make You Happy – Billy Woods
I've Got to Have Your Love – Pierre Hunt
Never Gonna Let You Go – Jobell and the Orchestra de Salsa
I'm So Glad I Found You – Linda Jones and the Whatnauts
Your Autumn of Tomorrow – The Crow
Manifesto – James Lewis and The Case of Time
Cochise – Paul Humphrey
You've Got to Try Harder – Ronnie Walker
I'm Com'un Home in the Morn'un – Lou Pride
Never Die – Mandrill
Tell Me Why – Life
Let Me Be Your Full Time Groover – Bill Brandon and Lorraine Johnson
If I Had My Way – Troy Keyes
Footsteps in the Shadows – Jimmy Jackson and the Kantlose Orchestra
Long Gone – Debbie Fleming
Feel the Need in Me – Graham Central Station
Control Tower – Magic Disco Machine
Disco Connection – Isaac Hayes
The Zoo (The Human Zoo) – The Commodores
I'm Learning to Trust My Man – Sisters Love
Nine Times – The Moments
Helplessly – Moment of Truth
Halos are for Angels – Blanch Carter
Move on Up – Curtis Mayfield
Can't Live Without You Baby – Connie Laverne
Supership – George Benson
Where is the Love – Betty Wright
Compared to What – Mr Flood's Party
Hey America – James Brown
Time – Edwin Starr
A House for Sale – Millie Jackson
Sending My Best Wishes – Garland Green
You Sexy Sugar Plum (But I Like It) – Roger Collins
Let Our Love Grow Higher – Eula Cooper
Uptown Saturday Night – Bill Harris

That list, plus the records mentioned in the above paragraphs, amounts to around a hundred 1970s records played in Northern Soul clubs of various sorts. I should say, I have tried my best to be certain that all of these are 70s releases, but given the obscurity of some tracks and the many re-releases, it is just possible the odd late-60s track may have crept in. If so: my apologies. However, there are many more 70s tracks that I have not listed, including Ian Levine's several made-for-the-scene records, and the point is well made: that 70s music was an intrinsic part of the Northern Soul scene and it is a myth that it was not.

Also noteworthy is the fact that a couple of these tracks actually use the term 'disco' in the song or band name. It must be a real bind for those who want Northern Soul to have nothing to do with disco to notice that 'Control Tower' by Magic Disco Machine is actually a Motown track and is produced by Northern Soul legend Frank Wilson, and that 'Disco Connection' is by another Soul hero, Isaac Hayes, and both are staggeringly good records that sent the dancefloors wild at many a Northern Soul all-nighter.

The following anecdote illustrates the idiocy that occurs when Northern Soul devotees try to build strict walls around their music to isolate it from funk, disco and the rest: someone had posted a James Brown track in the Northern Soul group on Facebook. This triggered a row between those who thought it should not be there and those who supported it, because of perceptions of James Brown and his music. Perhaps inevitably, someone wrote "James Brown is funk – end of story". At this blockheaded intervention, we were all presumably supposed to accept – since this was the "end of story" and no further discussion could be valid – that James Brown only made one kind of music and it was funk and we should not listen to him because it was unthinkable that he might have recorded a straightforward 4/4 beat dance track of a sort that would be acceptable in a Northern Soul club. In point of fact, James Brown had a career that spanned 6 decades, during which he made a wide variety of music, including Blues, Soul ballads, funk, disco and music that suited, and was played at, Northern Soul clubs. His game-changing 'Papa's Got a Brand New Bag' was played at Mod and proto-Northern Soul clubs. Admittedly, its jerky beat would not make it a favourite at later clubs, once Northern Soul established its identity. However, his 'There Was a Time' and 'Hey America' did have a proper 'Northern Soul' beat and were big sounds at various Northern Soul clubs. Moreover, there is another version of 'There Was a Time', by Gene Chandler, which was also massive at Northern Soul clubs. It is almost identical to James Brown's version, if a little faster, and no-one would think for a moment of calling it 'funk'. For our "end of story" guy, it seems understandings of 'funk' and 'Northern Soul' depend not on the way a record sounds but on whom it is by – the mindless application of labels is everything. The thing is, however, that that view – that anything associated with funk or disco or anything else that might not be 'true' Northern Soul has to be ejected from the Northern Soul canon, possibly without even hearing it and possibly without knowing that it has been a major Northern Soul hit – is not unique to that individual. The scene is awash with such ill-informed opinions expressed vehemently as facts. And these desperate views tend not only to skew the reality of the breadth of music played historically at Northern Soul clubs, they tend toward limiting the ability of the scene to really encompass all that it might. A decade on from Northern Soul's heyday and two decades on from 'Papa's Got a Brand New Bag', the great man made another record that should have graced any Northern Soul dancefloor: 'Living in America'. I don't know if any Northern Soul club has played it, but I do think minds and ears should open sufficiently to do so.

There is no distinct 'Northern Soul' sound. When a scene embraces acts as diverse as Mel Tormé, Gil Scott Heron and Diana Ross and the Supremes, how could there be? It was always a mongrel body of music, but one that centred on danceable black American music; as such it necessarily overlapped with disco and shared many of the same records. Northern Soul set out by playing new and recent records and was still doing so in the 1970s. The myth that Northern Soul was 60s-only seems to have come from various impulses. Firstly, the huge numbers that went to Wigan Casino when it took Northern Soul over ground found themselves in a club that was pulling up the drawbridge and trying to maintain a narrow view of the music, which focused mainly on the 1960s. Thus, many people got their initial (and sometimes only) immersion into the scene when it was already stuck in the past, and never saw it as forward-looking. This creates a slightly ironic situation, in which many of the older punters knew the scene as one that renewed itself with new music, and many of this bunch have continued to develop their taste throughout their lives, whilst some younger revellers insist that only the earlier music is valid and will have nothing to do with what they perceive as 'modern' Soul. Secondly, the name 'Northern Soul' created, in the minds of some, a distinct body of music that had its own style and boundaries, and that closed out certain things (and meant the demise of the scene, or at least its ossification). This meant the imposition of 'rules' about what was and wasn't Northern Soul, which were as incoherent as they were vehemently argued for. Thirdly, the Blackpool Mecca scene, in an equal-and-opposite reaction, eventually ejected Northern Soul from its playlists, so the old-and-new ethos that the original Northern Soul scene was founded on wasn't available there either, and that body of music became defined as something other than Northern Soul. Fourthly, there was a desire to separate out Northern Soul from 'disco', partly out of possessiveness and snobbery; partly because disco genuinely was a different scene overall, notwithstanding the overlaps and shared music; and partly because disco fell into disrepute when the mainstream got hold of it and the association became intolerable.

There may well also be a case for saying that, by the mid-70s, black American dance music makers – acts like Chic, Earth Wind and Fire, The O'Jays and the rest, and their various songwriters, producers, backing musicians etc. – had become so utterly accomplished at what they did that the only way Northern Soul could compete and maintain its distance was through obdurate militancy, rather than any convincing aural, critical or stylistic argument.

# Everybody was leaping about, doing backdrops and spins and that....

Er, no. That's not true either. This is another aspect of the scene as much generated by as exposed by the media.

Demonstrative moves, such as backdrops, front-drops, spins and combinations of these have become part of Northern Soul's folklore, but as with so much in this, the truth is different from the hype. It is fair to say that, historically, some people did do those gymnastic moves, and there is some precedence for the activity to draw on – possibly in James Brown's and Jackie Wilson's expressive stage performances, which involved sometimes spins and dropping to the knees – but it was always a minority interest.

The first time I saw some semblance of those kinds of moves was in about 1970: a skinhead at The Moon was on the dancefloor, showing off to a couple of girls and doing a few moves to a Reggae beat. The display culminated in his throwing himself forward, onto his palms, doing a couple of press-ups, then simulating copulation. The Reggae beat seemed quite well suited to this purpose. One or two of my friends, including one a bit older than me who'd been a regular at The Twisted Wheel, would do the odd spin and backdrop, but it was occasional and understated. During The Torch era, but at one of my local clubs – Druffies, in Dukinfield – an individual, let's call him M, was trying out a few extravagant moves on the dancefloor. He took off, apparently planning a front-drop, and was horizontal in the air about four feet from the ground, arms and legs in the sort of position a skydiver adopts, when he was apparently distracted and lost sight of what it was he intended to do. He dropped to the ground, still in the same position, shattering teeth on the parquet flooring.

Although it is evident, even looking way back, that a few people would occasionally do these moves, it's hard to imagine there being enough room on a tiny dancefloor like that at like the Wheel or at the usually rammed Torch for many to indulge the full-on leaping and diving that became relatively popular later. In the 'When was Northern Soul?' section, above, I reproduce a tract from Hinkley Soul Club, which describes acrobatic dancing first being seen at the Twisted Wheel in about 1969, and other dancers stopping to watch. This is indicative of the novelty of the practice and perhaps of the fact that if one or two were doing this, everyone else on the dancefloor would be so bunched together that they couldn't dance anyway. Wigan Casino, however, was a much bigger club with a much bigger dancefloor. This and a combination of other factors seem to have gelled to foster this activity.

There had been dancing competitions at The Torch, but they were a minor thing there, and the practice took off in a much bigger way at Wigan Casino. Also, the Casino's large dancefloor encouraged and facilitated more extravagant moves, whether people were formally competing or not. Bruce Lee movies and records like Carl Douglas's 'Kung Fu Fighting' (which wasn't played on the Northern Soul scene, by the way – wrong sort of sound), meant that high-kicking martial arts were part of the zeitgeist. The media paid no attention to any Northern Soul club until Wigan Casino – apart from the odd salacious local newspaper tale about drug busts – but when the programme makers made their way into the place, they were naturally most interested in the most spectacular aspects of the scene, and those were of course the dancefloor calisthenics. The media made the leaping and diving the key feature of the scene – ahead of the music – for the lay public, even though most who attended didn't do it. Even now, when I mention the scene to people who were not involved, the first thing they ask about is the acrobatic dancing. Because the media highlighted these performances and broadcast them to millions, the impression was given that that's what everyone did, so more did it. Coachloads arrived at the doors of Wigan Casino and newcomers poured in through the doors to watch or have a crack at that kind of dancing.

Even then, it remained a minority interest. If you look at the footage, overall, of the dancefloor at Wigan Casino, back in the 70s, most of the dancers are just dancing. I have never done a backdrop in my life and very few of my friends have.

Whereas the gymnastic dancing trend and the accompanying dancing competitions that gained prominence in the mid-70s suited some, they were for many a kind of sell-out and an irritation. Conspicuous display and presenting your skills for scrutiny in competitions were at odds with what Northern Soul had been to this point. Dancing at Soul clubs was originally a self-derived, anarchic, bottom-up thing for which no-one sought or gave approval. But, whereas there were no rules, it is fair to say that there was a kind of loose understanding that some dancing fitted the bill better than some other dancing – there was the concept of the 'good dancer' and therefore of the 'not-very-good dancer'. However, this was an informal and understated thing. People learned to dance from just doing it and from watching others, so they ended up with something that was partly in keeping with the scene and the music, but that was also partly their own. The presence of a dance competition, however, implied submission to some sort of higher authority, which had the knowledge and status to judge how well you did it. And trying to perfect all those leaps and dives was to allow media and mainstream interference to influence what had previously been free and spontaneous. This was the opposite of the rapturous notion that you should 'always dance like there's no-one else there'. Now dancing was to be done as though someone was both watching and evaluating. That hands over the right to someone to make that judgment, and it implies and permits the creation of qualitative and stylistic rules. The outlook of many on the scene toward the mid-70s outbreak of gymnastic dancing is captured well by my friend from the Midlands who described what was going on at Wigan Casino as a 'circus'. That seems not an unreasonable analogy for dancing that has made the transition from an internal pleasure – a rapturous private engagement with music in a public place – to display for public consumption. How dance competitions were perceived by some is well captured by the movie *Northern Soul*, when the core characters meet the idea with dismay and ridicule: a character who has won a tacky looking trophy for dancing is told to do himself a favour and get rid of it because it is an embarrassment.[38] There is also the practical or maybe health-and-safety issue, that it is not a comfortable thing to have some bloke dancing near you suddenly launch a size nine up to within inches of your face. I say all this whilst recognising that many love their gymnastic dancing, as they have every right to. My point is this: that the broad public exposure of Northern Soul has created the myth that this was what everyone did. It wasn't – most didn't do it and many had the negative responses to it I describe above. As with much that this book describes, the change occurred as Northern Soul went over ground. New arrivals, seeing the scene in this particular phase and condition, would have seen gymnastic dancing and dance competitions as normal and would have been unlikely to recognise the contradictions set out above.

Dance competitions have become a feature of major current Northern Soul events, like the scene's various weekenders, and often it seems that the endeavour on the part of the protagonists is to include the greatest number of the most extravagant moves. And it therefore seems to be the case that those

---

[38] Northern Soul. (2014) Film. Dir. Elaine Constantine

best geared for those competitions aren't just people who turn up to dance, but those who work out, possibly do martial arts and train and practice like a specialist. Indeed, one of Wigan Casino's champion dancers was also a Thai Kickboxing champion. This has meant that, to a degree, and for some, the gymnastic moves have become foregrounded, and dancing to, or interpreting, the music has become incidental. Looking at dance competitions on YouTube, there are embarrassing bits of footage of some individuals leaping, kicking and doing the splits almost in defiance of what's coming out of the loudspeakers. I hasten to add, however, that this is not always so and there are some great dancers who clearly are engaged with the music.

However, it remains the case that this aspect of the scene has been magnified and distorted by media interest and by those who are influenced by such things, and that the vast majority of attendees at Northern Soul events still don't do any of those fancy moves; they just stay on their feet and dance to the music they adore, as was always the case.

# Rarity, Divs and Handbaggers

I will argue, below, in the section 'Mouldy Oldies' that a perception that there is resentment among those who have been on the scene for ages against newcomers is a misconception and that there is no Northern Soul elite, as such, and no specific resentment against people on the basis that they are new to the scene. However, as with any walk of life, there are groups who create arbitrary rules in order to differentiate themselves from others – 'others' who do not know, or fail to adhere to, these 'rules'. We define our identities partly by whom we are not, and we point-up perceived characteristics or flaws in others and bolster our egos by making it known that we do not have those characteristics or flaws, and we take pleasure and comfort in group-bonding with the like-minded, at the expense of 'others' whom we hold to be inferior.[39] In the Northern Soul scene, this generally turns not on newness to the scene, but on knowledge of the scene and its expectations, the rarity of records and (as further explored in the Mouldy Oldies section, below), on whether or not someone indulges in Northern Soul's dress-code clichés.

Rare records were always a part of the Northern Soul scene. This is pretty much an inevitability, as the scene developed as one which played records that had never been released in the UK or, if they had, were now deleted and hard to find. The indifference to this music on the part of the general populace in the UK in the mid 60s meant that even if a record had been released here, there would be few copies in circulation. There are of course a few exceptions – some Soul tracks did make the top forty – but most went unnoticed and only found their way into the hands of DJs, clubbers and Soul collectors.

Clearly, there is pleasure to be had in owning something rare and beautiful – a pleasure well known among art and antique collectors. For some, it ends

---

[39] See references to Husserl, p.617 in Bullock, A., Stallybrass, O., Trombley, S. The Fontana Dictionary of Modern Thought. Fontana, London. 1988

there: to get hold of a rare 1960s 7" disc that has been longed-for for ages is a pretty good feeling, and placing it on the turntable and hearing that wonderful music and knowing you've got it and can play it any time, and can maybe make your friends a little envious, are all that matters. Plus, there is that well-known phenomenon of DJs back in Northern Soul's heyday wanting to keep records rare, sometimes by covering-up song titles and singers and substituting invented alternatives, to keep punters coming through the door at their particular club. But things have mutated and now go further than that.

With Northern Soul having gone substantially over ground, there are far more collectors and DJs now than there have ever been. This means that a cache of records which were already rare is spread even more thinly. There are two key effects of this.

Firstly, the less knowledgeable DJs and collectors only know of the least rare records, so the endless replaying of the same old played-out records is something frowned upon by those who know of or own rarer records. A couple of anecdotes will help illustrate the impact of this: a social-media spat rolls on in the East Manchester towns I grew up in (though no doubt the equivalent goes on in many places), between various individuals on the two sides of this argument: one side berates the other for only being interested in the same tired old records; the other berates the first lot for presiding over tedious events, where no-one has heard any of the music and the dancefloor is largely empty. I was at an event some time ago, also, coincidentally, in East Manchester, when an old associate – let's call him 'X' – who hadn't danced all night suddenly jumped up onto an otherwise largely empty floor and danced with great gusto to one rather uninteresting record. A stranger standing next to me recognised the confusion on my face and leant over to explain: "X only dances to records worth more than £300". One can see the one-upmanship working in both ways in this: the rare record enthusiast regards the rare record as part of his cultural capital. It could be that he owns this particular disc, or just that he wants to signal that he knows it. Either way, he endeavours to distinguish himself from 'the Other' by signalling his cultural (and maybe financial) investment in the rare record; the deadpan observer recognises and quietly mocks the performance he sees, and shares it with what he takes to be a fellow sceptic. It should also be added, however, that X might reasonably like the record and enjoy dancing to it. Having said that, however, it does seem to me that some of the current crop of rare records would not have made the grade back in the day and only get spun because the bar has been lowered to accommodate them. I recognise the subjectivity in this, but there is also a certain inevitability in the good records being used up first and there then being a certain amount of head-scratching over which of those left can reasonably be played. Though it is also the case that records have continued to be discovered since the scene's heyday and their not having been played before is not necessarily based on quality, but on their unavailability.

Secondly, great controversy rages around the provenance of records. The Northern Soul scene is inundated with 'bootleg' or counterfeit records, often now known as 'boots', for short. This dates right back to the beginning of the 1970s, when the scene became an identifiable entity, and the demand for records markedly outstripped supply. The first bootlegs made little or no attempt to emulate the originals. A UK-based bootlegger created a label called 'Soul Sounds', which produced on thick, heavy vinyl with a fixed centre, records which only previously existed as open-centred American imports.[40] Soul Sounds discs looked more or less like routine UK pressings, but with little of the usual additional information beyond the singer and song, like release date, arranger, producer etc.. Other labels, like 'Out of the Past' (or 'OOTP'), looked like proper American imports, whilst the labels themselves were bogus and of course not the labels the originals were on. However, other bootleggers made efforts to make their records look just like the original. Given that these records were pressed in the US for the UK market, they had the 'feel' of proper imports. And whereas some such pressings are easily spotted, others are so good that the only way to tell is by close scrutiny of the graphics or, in the most extreme cases, by looking at the serial number etched into the 'dead wax' – the plain bit containing the run-out groove, between the playing area and the label – even then, you need to know what ought to be there in order to know whether what's actually there is kosher.

Back in Northern Soul's heyday, mail-order record dealers sold bootlegs alongside proper imports, and many record buyers would have bought bootlegs without knowing it. Others bought bootlegs with few qualms about the ethics of doing so, or about not paying the makers of the record for their work. The views at work in this are complex.

In the circumstances of the time, it was largely working-class teenagers, living for the moment, who were buying these records. This was not a group who would have given much thought to intellectual property – in the unlikely event that they'd actually even heard the term – or record company royalties. Speaking as someone who was one of those teenagers, the world appeared in shades of 'us' and 'them': 'us' being friends and family and maybe one or two trusted people at work; 'them' being that great amorphous mass of things and people that impacted on our lives but were beyond our reach and our

---

[40] Sometimes these records had been released in the UK in the mid-60s, on labels like Stateside and United Artists before being deleted and becoming rare and in-demand, but the fact remains that Soul Sounds looked nothing like even these labels.

ken. 'Them' was name for the place where products and laws and everything else came from. It was our task to do and get what we wanted from this thing, whilst avoiding its wrath and sanctions. And bearing in mind that the Northern Soul scene existed on the margins and was powered to a significant extent by illicit drugs, usually stolen from pharmacies, ethics were already low on most people's priorities. That a thing had been paid for was ethics enough – where the money went was out of sight and out of mind. The only time ethics would be likely to arise would be if someone were a serious collector and had paid for and expected an original.

Moreover, there was also the feeling that if the record companies failed to make records available, they only had themselves to blame. Many Northern Soul fans would have loved an original copy of a record, but would settle for the bootleg if it was the only option. It was seldom the case that a bootleg was bought in preference to an original; it was usually that there were no copies of the original to be had, or that what few there were were almost impossible to find and then far too expensive for most pockets. When there are tens of thousands of Northern Soul fans and only a handful of original copies of a record, something has to give, and it was the bootleggers who filled that gap and made the profit, if the copyright owners failed to step up.

If that was the 1970s, a new morality has now emerged, which makes itself heard on social media. I refer to the phenomenon of 'OVO': Original Vinyl Only. Many clubs and DJs now proudly tout themselves as playing OVO. OVO-ists seek an ethical high-ground by insisting on the primacy of the original vinyl record. Many OVO clubs have deck cams (video cameras that point at the turntables and project the image onto a large screen), so that punters can save themselves from the ignominy of dancing to the wrong pressing of a record.

I engaged an OVO DJ in conversation on Facebook to hear his position on this. He saw his position as an ethical one, in that only by buying an original does one pay royalties back to the artist and record company. This argument seems reasonable at first, but the logic comes apart somewhat on closer inspection. Firstly, most Northern Soul records were made in the 1960s or the first half of the 1970s, and many of the artists who made them are now dead. The session musicians – what few may be still alive – would have been paid for the session at the time, and the matter is closed for them. Secondly, many Northern Soul records are so obscure that even if an artist were still alive, trying to track him/her down to hand over royalties might be an impossible task. Similarly, whereas record and licensing companies would still quite rightly expect their fee on the sale of a record, many of the labels that put out those 60s and 70s sounds were obscure and are now lost to history. This also connects to the biggest hole in this particular argument: that these records have already been sold once or turned into bulk trade sales and dumped in warehouses. So, even if the record company that pressed the original disc is still around and still owns the rights to the music, their interest in the sale was concluded decades ago. Sales of these records, now, are sales of second-hand discs, and royalties do not apply. Northern Soul records now trade, in some cases, for thousands of pounds. This does not go to the artist or record company; it goes only to the seller. Even though bootlegs are fundamentally ethically wrong, this knocks the royalties argument into a cocked hat.

I put it to the OVO-ist that a DJ might face a situation where he s/he wanted to play a record to his/her audience, but could only get a non-original copy; and I suggested that in these circumstances the DJ might be justified in playing a non-original copy, because the alternative was not to play it at all. The OVO-ist's position on this was that if you do not have the original of a record, you should not use a substitute source – not even a legal one – you should play an altogether different record instead. This means, then, that from an OVO DJ's perspective, you may want to play a tune, you may know your audience would be enraptured to hear it, and you could get it on a non-original platter – indeed, you may already own on a non-original platter – but you do not, on principle, play it; you play another record, which is, by definition, a second choice. I will leave you, dear reader, to decide on the sense of that position.

The OVO supporter also made the point that punters on the dancefloor are being sold short if a DJ plays a bootleg, because of sound quality. In nearly 5 decades of attending Northern Soul clubs, I can't say that sound quality has ever been an issue. Back in the scene's heyday, there would be distortion from widely variable sound systems, plus the noise of punters pounding the dancefloor and bellowing in order to hold conversations over the often ear-splitting volume of the speakers, so imperfect sound was normal and no-one gave it a second thought. Even if sound quality were an issue now, that would be no reason to say that the original disc would be better than an official rerelease. Moreover, whilst it is true that some bootlegs are of pretty awful quality, others display little or no noticeable sonic difference from an original. And, indeed, some original 1960s pressings can be iffy, or worn, which means that a re-engineered rerelease can actually be better. This takes me onto the next point.

OVO-ists also set their faces against compact discs and re-released vinyl discs – official pressings where the licence holders would get their fee and the sound quality might be even better than on a 1960s pressing. In a further Facebook exchange, another OVO-ist explained his position on this: when he had paid an exorbitant sum for an original vinyl record, he did not want to mount the stage to do his set after some other twonk had spun the same tune on Grapevine (a properly accountable re-release label).[41]

So there we have it: OVO comes from what appears to be a high ethical ground, but ultimately it is about protectionism. Whilst it is understandable that many collectors logically and reasonably want the original of a record because it is the original, the translation of this private passion into a kind of public ethical crusade is not without its attendant issues, its effect on the market being one.

In another interesting exchange between OVO-ists on social media, various individuals teased each other affably over the fact that many own bootlegs from before the moment they saw the light and became confirmed OVO-ists. They also discussed the fact that some sell their old bootlegs in order to divest their collections of the taint, presumably once they have been able to get hold of an original, though possibly some just sell them on the principle that bootlegs are wicked and should not be owned or as part of the routine trading process that goes on between collectors. The problem is that bootlegs, though nowhere near as valuable as originals, still have some value, and few would be so principled as to destroy a bootleg in preference to selling it on. So, in part, at least, the OVO-ists are the source of the bootlegs they condemn buyers for buying – the social media exchange I described did include OVO-ists playfully calling each other 'hypocrites'. There would be a caveat to this, however, as from an OVO perspective, owning bootlegs is not as damnable as playing them out (playing them to a public audience), so there is the conscience-salving thought that the bootleg has been sold in the expectation of only personal use, though clearly there is no way of knowing of or controlling this.

There are of course only a limited number of original pressings around, and as the pressure only to play an original grows, prices rise. This has the effect of making the OVO-ists' collections ever more valuable, and of making it harder for a new, outsider DJ to get started, if s/he observes the OVO code. Meanwhile, those who don't follow the OVO code are persistently condemned by OVO-ists in social media. Such is the pressure to get it right, many now put images of their records onto Facebook and ask others to vet them: is this an original? How can we tell? What are the distinguishing features? Is it OK to play this one out? On the same pages, wrongdoers trying

---

[41] To give some context: I recently saw a copy of 'This Won't Change' by Lester Tipton on its original 1966 American 'La Beat' record label sold on an auction site for £4,600. 'Grapevine' label copies, pressed legitimately in the UK in 1980, are currently offered online for between £5 and £30. For £7.99 you can buy a CD containing this and 29 other tracks.

to sell old bootlegs on Ebay and other selling sites are exposed and castigated.

There are bizarre anomalies. There exists the phenomenon of the 'carver': one can send an MP3 file or compact disc to a company that will cut a vinyl 45 for you from it for about £15. This, it seems, is legal, because you have paid for the tune in the first place. It would seem, however, that this would only be so if one does not sell the record on, in the same way that home taping of your own records onto a cassette was, if it was just for your own use; but if you started running off copies for your mates, you were effectively a bootlegger. Thus, one nervous new DJ, wondering what to do when he wanted to play out a tune that he could only get on CD, was advised via someone on social media to have a carver made and to play that, but to take the CD with him to demonstrate, should he be challenged on the matter, that he had at some point paid for a legitimate recording.

Another unintended consequence is that a boxful of original vinyl records, at current prices – hundreds or thousands of pounds for one single – can easily be worth more than a brand new luxury car, and having them set out by the decks in a busy nightclub is rather like leaving a Porsche parked with the keys in and might be an unnerving experience for some DJs.

The OVO phenomenon, then, has set up a clear dichotomy in Northern Soul: one crowd who sees their devotion to original records as a kind of ethical guardianship of authenticity, even if the flipside of this is a form of protectionism; and another, which sees its ethical high ground as existing in the idea that it's the music that counts and the medium it comes from is of limited importance.

Given that accruing a good collection of original rare records might take a lifetime – and, at today's prices, a vast amount of money – it is often the case that OVO-ists are from earlier generations of Northern Soul collectors. As such, they might, in addition to looking down on players of rereleases, bootlegs, CDs and MP3s, not hold in particularly high regard those who express their interest in Northern Soul through its clichés, like dressing up in reproduction mid-1970s baggy trousers. But then this does not only apply to OVO-ists; many older people on the scene – whether they have great record collections or not – and some younger ones too, also object to the banalities through which Northern Soul is now represented in public, and are scornful of those individuals who play along with the rituals. For more on this see 'Mouldy Oldies', below.

This takes me on to the 'handbagger', but before I examine that phenomenon, a word on the connected notion of the 'div'.

'Div' was a term used back in the 70s to describe an individual who didn't 'get it', usually through being new to the scene or just not getting involved enough to understand how things worked. A div might get the fashions wrong, might follow unquestioningly the scene's more outlandish practices, s/he might not understand 'cool', he or she might be seduced by and be disproportionately interested in the scene's peripheral aspects and get no deeper, his/her behaviour might be immature and embarrassing, and s/he would probably be unable to distinguish between the records the cognoscenti would regard highly and those they would not. In particular, the div might be into the records that had been rereleased or played-out or become widely available on bootlegs or readily-available imports and spun in youth clubs.

Now, when those of who were around in Northern Soul's heyday are middle-aged or older, the use of the word 'div' is less comfortable. We have mellowed and are less judgmental – publicly, at least – and are not as prone to bullying and name-calling as our juvenile selves. Nevertheless, the term still does occasionally crop up, particularly on social media, when the user of the term is usually playing to a like-minded crowd and screened by the relative anonymity afforded by the medium. The following is typical: someone will put up footage of a crowd of baggy-trousered, badge-bedecked men and women in their 40s and 50s, dancing in some public square to some flogged-to-death Northern Soul track – 'Do I love You' or 'The Night', usually – and scores of contributors will express their contempt in the comments column, and the term 'div' is almost certain to appear. The way the critics feel was captured well in a recent such post, where footage of the sort described had been modified to comic effect: the Northern Soul track had been erased and in its place was the nursery-rhyme tune 'Teddy Bears' Picnic', played on what sounded like ice-cream-van bells. The fact that the newly overdubbed tune seemed to fit perfectly with the dancers' rhythm added to the comic effect.

It is not only those who most spiritedly engage with Northern Soul's visible clichés who come in for scorn: those who latched briefly onto Northern Soul in the 1970s and believed the dodgy white pop records through which Northern Soul came to the public ear to be Soul music – and maybe even the zenith of Northern Soul – would have been thought 'divs' by many back then. And even if, today, many would shy away from that word, they would still be scornful of those whose tastes centre on, or include, this music. However, there is more to this snobbery than just having a negative view of those who view the scene through this kind of music, as it does not just look down on naff, non-Soul records, but on what were once great Soul records but are now played out. In other words, the snobbery ceases to be about the music, but about access to it and knowledge of it.

In the contemporary milieu, the handbagger has replaced the div. Another disparaging term, it obviously comes from the 60s/70s cliché of girls dancing around their handbags. I'm not sure anyone still does that, but the term is still used, regardless, to describe those who don't understand Northern Soul etiquette. For there to be a crowd of people considered 'divs' or 'handbaggers', there has to be another group who sees them that way. As shorthand, I will refer to these as 'Northern Soul's cognoscenti'. These might be OVO-ists; record collectors of long standing, without necessarily much of an OVO bias; individuals who have been on the scene from way back, and might not be particularly interested in collecting records, but dislike the commercialisation that has squatted on it (see 'Mouldy Oldies' for more on this); and later arrivals who nevertheless find themselves drawn to the characteristics of the scene in its earlier phases and similarly seek to disown the clichés and commercialisation which are now part-and-parcel of it. It should also be said, however, that there are people from all eras of the scene who are also highly knowledgeable about Northern Soul but do not care too much about handbaggers and what they do, or about the scene's clichés and commercialisation. These people too are clearly cognoscenti. However, for the purposes of this discourse, the cognoscenti I refer to are only the ones who are irritated by the aspects I describe.

The current rise in popularity of Northern Soul has resulted in a large number of new people coming to the scene, including, no doubt, many older people who heard Northern Soul's top ten at the youth club back in the 70s and 80s and want to hear those records again, and those who have picked up on Northern Soul's now unavoidable public presence and want to give it a try. So there is a new set of tensions between the cognoscenti and the handbaggers.

The handbagger's social indiscretions overlap with those of the div, but are not quite identical. They come in four areas: taking drinks onto the dancefloor, using talcum powder (talc) on the dancefloor, liking only the top few Northern Soul tracks and indulging in Northern Soul's clichés.

Northern Soul is about dancing, so it is important that the dance floor is in good order. If it gets wet in places, it becomes sticky and difficult to dance on; a substantial amount of wet on a dancefloor might even be dangerous. No serious Northern Soul punter would take a drink onto the dancefloor. Handbaggers, however, frequently fail to observe this piece of etiquette, and mess and irritation for others tend to follow.

The use of talc to make dancefloors skiddier is a bone of contention. It is one of those aspects of the scene made by media of various sorts to seem almost obligatory, and some therefore expect to use it whenever they dance. But many of Northern Soul's cognoscenti object to it, and someone using talc is likely to be considered a handbagger. Some venues ban talc. There was even, for a time, a Northern Soul group on Facebook called 'No Talc', so that those who disapproved of talc could exchange stories and express their outrage at its use, though that group seems to have vanished now. Logically, objectively, one would think there is a common-sense middle-ground: if the dancefloor is sticky, the use of talc will probably help; if it isn't, you don't need it. But, whatever the case, there's no need to throw it around on principle, or as though doing so is some sort of devotional rite – certain photographers may have some responsibility here, in that a flying spread of talc has been used at times for dramatic effect in photographs of Northern Soul dancers – but equally, it seems churlish to get on someone's case if a sticky dancefloor is ruining their evening and a bit of talc would help. Some have pulled the argument into one of perceived real practicalities or health and safety issues: club owners might not want white footprints trailing over the carpeted areas, whilst some think that talc, when airborne, might hinder asthmatics. Given that, used judiciously, it should stay on or near the ground; that dirt from outside and spilt drinks are likely to be trod all over the place; that there is usually a gauntlet of smokers to run, to get in and out of a club; and that one might take in a lung-full of aerosol deodorant when getting ready for such a night out, all of this looks to a degree like instrumental reasoning and an effort to apply a constructed ethical principle around a private or group prejudice. However, it is the case that some use talc extravagantly and that does cause real problems – see below.

Tension exists between the cognoscenti and the handbaggers (and others) over playlists. Oversimplifying things, but creating a starting point: one side wants to play and hear rare and underplayed music; the other wants to hear well-known Northern Soul tunes. I refer to an example of this tension in paragraphs above, amongst music listeners in clubs in East Manchester. Interestingly, one of those vociferously arguing for the well-known music was someone I know to have been on the scene from the mid-70s. I can also report that I have attended the Twisted Wheel revival sessions in Manchester many times over the last few years, and seen the place crammed with people of all ages, including old Wheelers who still want to dance to the music of their youth. So it is not just handbaggers who like to hear those songs from the classic era of the scene, and the situation is by no means black and white.

However, positions do become polarised: some clubs will stick solely to rare and underplayed music, so that anyone rolling up for a good night out dancing to much-loved Northern Soul will find themselves hearing nothing they know. Conversely, one might show up at a handbagger event and find oneself hearing nothing but the most tired old records.

There is also the issue, mentioned above, that some rare records aren't terribly good. Rarity does not confer quality. In relation to this, the disparaging term 'beard-strokers' has cropped up on social media, in an effort on the part of some to fight back against the cognoscenti. Beard-strokers might be defined as those who take a connoisseur's approach to listening to music, thoughtfully considering the merits of each exquisitely rare record. However, beard-strokers are as alien to the original spirit of Northern Soul as the screeching, blind-drunk handbagger, who is only at a Northern Soul club because someone at work reckoned it's a good night out, and would be as happy dancing to Abba, Bon Jovi or Robbie Williams.

Back in Northern Soul's heyday, the best clubs mixed things up: well-known tunes were interspersed with new finds and new releases. It was a great formula for giving everyone the thrill of dancing to their favourite tunes and keeping the scene alive by bringing in the new. It is also possible, even now, to put together substantial playlist of music which is good and reasonably well-known, but which excludes the most played-out records. However, it is also fair to say that what is reasonably well-known and what is overplayed is very much a matter of personal perspective, turning on how much each individual has stayed involved with the scene. Someone who was deeply involved in the scene way back, but has dipped out for a long period, might be happy to hear records that someone who has remained closely involved throughout might not. So this gives us two kinds of cognoscenti, at odds with each other.

One would have to imagine that between the handbaggers and the cognoscenti, there is a huge grey area of people with diverse views on the commercialisation and self-parodying of the scene, including those who reverse the logic, i.e.: there will be some who have been around for ages and don't mind it, and those who are new to the scene but already have distaste for it. However, regardless of how we identify the loci of these different views, this polarisation does exist. So again, for ease of communication, even if the terms are leaky and not especially satisfactory, I will use 'handbaggers' and 'cognoscenti' to describe how the two sides in this dichotomy are perceived in views made public, in social media in particular.

The cognoscenti sneer at the endless stream of Northern Soul tat that comes onto the market, whilst the undiscerning/handbaggers lap it up. The cognoscenti show up at Soul dos wearing more or less what they'd wear to work or the pub; the others arrive in their baggies, circle skirts and other items regarded as necessary Northern Soul wear. Some oldies wear skinhead gear or tonic suits in order to make an alternative statement and eschew the baggy-trouser cliché. Interestingly, however, no-one wears the fashions that came immediately after the baggies look – the A-line flared trouser with cheesecloth shirt, for example, or the tapered 'peg' trouser and cap-sleeve T-shirt – so efforts to challenge the 'Northern Soul look' have, it seems, to involve something that came before. This may be to define the wearer as someone who not only rejects the baggy-trouser cliché, but is either from an earlier era, or identifies with that earlier era and its values. But it is not just these more palpable aspects that define the different groups. Old footage from mid-70s Wigan Casino shows the faces of amphetamine-fuelled revellers as they feel the combined high of the drug and the music; this phenomenon was made much more visible when it was portrayed by actors in the movie *Northern Soul*; and now dancers who have never seen a green-and-clear in their lives include, periodically, as part of their dance routine, that ecstatic stare and facial expression.

What appears to be at stake in this game of identity politics is authenticity. The cognoscenti believe they have it; the handbaggers and other kinds of 'others' seek it through buying tokens of it and proudly displaying them; the cognoscenti resent the phoniness of this new facsimile of 'their' scene, even though, in truth, their late-60s/early-70s scene borrowed significantly from the first-time-around early-60s Mods. Some cognoscenti assert their perceived authenticity by wearing pre-baggies fashions, though those styles too are widely copied. To add to the complexity, those who were part of the late-70s Mod revival – the era of The Selecter, The Specials et al – are also middle-aged now and may choose the tonic suit and/or skinhead look in order to identify with an era after Northern Soul's heyday. There is another aspect, I feel, at work in this, and that is the fact that baggy trousers and circle skirts may have been a tolerable look for emaciated 1970s, speed-freak teenagers – they do not work so well on the portly and middle-aged. The fact that someone chose to set footage of some such folk frolicking in the street to the tune 'The Teddy Bears' Picnic' might not only have been to parody indulgence in cliché, but to point up just how risible those fashions now look on those who no longer have the appropriate physique. Perhaps there should be some kind of coefficient relating the acceptable width of a person's baggies to their waist measurement.

The following anecdotes summarise my experience of a couple of Northern Soul events, peopled mostly by what I expect the cognoscenti would call handbaggers. They both took place on Saturday nights in small, provincial market towns, in the functions rooms of large, centrally placed pubs. The towns were quite some way apart and the events were separated by a couple of years.

I arrived at the first at about nine in the evening. The room was sparsely populated, but some of the few present were Soul aficionados I knew or half-knew from other events in the area, and the DJs seemed to be doing a decent job of mixing up the well-known with the not so well-known – the event had some promise. However, soon after my arrival, large numbers of people spilled in from the pub's main room. Most were the worse for drink, some were absolutely blotto, a few were scarcely in control of themselves and lurched and wobbled around, seemingly oblivious to where they were or what they were doing. The room was starting to take on the feel of a zombie flick. One woman, visibly out of her mind and staggering about on the dancefloor, was escorted from the room, but staggered back in several times, each time being escorted out again, until the escort finally gave up and the woman stayed and spent the next hour or so stumbling around the space, apparently aimlessly. Another exceedingly drunk woman veered around the room and eventually collapsed onto the turntables and interrupted the entertainment for a few minutes, as the jocks tried to get the sound working again. Others, not quite so worse for wear, swayed around with pint pots in their hands, doing a dance which involved limited movement, so as not to spill any beer, if possible. At some point, someone threw a large quantity of talc across the floor at about chest height. A few minutes later, someone else did the same from the other side. I could make no sense of this, as this was already the slippiest dancefloor I had been on in years – it really did not need talc. Dancing, soon afterwards, I could see talc hanging densely in the air, in the white rays aimed downward from the ceiling-slung spotlights. I was getting concerned, as I suffer from asthma. I tried to dance just breathing through my nose, to give myself at least some chance of keeping this stuff out of my lungs, but I still dance with a bit of gusto and need a substantial amount of air to keep going, so inevitably I opened my mouth and took in some gulps of it. A little while later, a woman in a black trouser suit walked onto the dancefloor, talc container in hand, and hurled huge quantities of it into the air. This time, chest height was not enough: she threw it up in extravagant arcs at the lights, for effect. The dancefloor was completely shrouded in a great white cloud of the stuff, to above head height, giving it the look of a freshly-shaken snow globe. I could clearly feel it getting on my chest, and I left. I was still coughing 48 hours later.

At the second such event, there was a band on, doing Northern Soul covers. The original Northern Soul scene was almost entirely a records-based affair. Live acts were few, and certainly cover bands were unheard of. A group of women all had on matching Northern Soul T-shirts, with the black fist logo and the exhortation to 'Keep the Faith'. I made my way onto the near-empty dancefloor, and as I got into the rhythm, I realised there was a perimeter of faces around the edge, watching what I was doing. I am not used to anyone paying attention to my dancing at Northern Soul dos. What I do is commonplace and of little interest to anyone, and at any usual such event I am used to being more or less invisible. It's not even as though I do backdrops, spins and such – I just dance. As the evening wore on, the dancefloor became ever more packed, until it was awash with roaring, falling-down drunks who, pint pot in hand, lurched backwards, forwards and sideways, spilling beer on the floor and colliding with their neighbours. Many of the dancers, particularly the males, evidently could not be seen to be dancing for dancing's sake and therefore had to mess about, bellowing at their friends making gestures of mutual and self-mockery. Whilst one could not say with certainty that no-one was there for, or was enjoying, the music, it is fair to say that nothing about the behaviour of this particular sub-group gave any sense that they had any interest in it, though they may, at some point in the future, look back nostalgically to this moment and say they were 'into' Northern Soul. And they may, in a decade or so's time – whenever Northern Soul undergoes its next revival – pull on a pair of baggies and a badge-covered singlet, to display their history within, and devotion to, the Northern Soul scene. They might even hold forth, with an authoritative tone, on how, back in its heyday, the scene was a drug-free and violence-free affair.

# Mouldy Oldies

There are two issues at stake here: firstly, the tension between the late-60s/early-70s crowd and those who arrived after the scene went over ground in the mid-70s; and secondly, that between more or less the same first bunch, plus some of the second, and those who revel in the public exposure Northern Soul now enjoys/endures in the current milieu. The former could be characterised, in an oversimplified way, but for convenience for now, as resentment that the scene went over ground and invited in lots of outsiders who changed the scene, and not for the better. The latter could be characterised as irritation at how the scene has become over-commercialised in recent times, amidst a plethora of trashy merchandising and parody, which has skewed perceptions of the scene. These things are, however, often conflated, perhaps with good reason, as those who object to the way things are now seem most likely be from that up-to-1974 underground era, and because the current phase of commercialisation could be seen as an echo of the mid-70s Wigan Casino-based one.

Northern Soul is currently bigger than it has ever been. This phenomenon is marked not only by a broader audience than ever for the music, but also by relentless crass marketing. References to Northern Soul are everywhere and more or less any thing can be marketed by attaching the words 'Northern Soul' to it, even, as we saw at the start of this book, a Tory Party conference.

As well as the predictable-enough T-shirts and badges, Northern Soul features in, or on, or is used to sell: key rings, hats, sports bags, hoodies, handbags, tea light holders, purses, mugs, bedspreads, coasters, baby bibs and rompers, lamps, eggs, dog jackets, oil paintings and prints thereof, lighters, wallets, cellphone covers, necklaces, flip-flops, greetings cards, umbrellas, books, calendars, cushion covers, pillow cases, movies, posters, bar towels, watches, clocks, socks, spare-wheel covers, cakes, cake stands, car stickers, mouse mats, chopping boards, breakfast cereals, wrapping paper, grilled cheese sandwiches, bracelets, pouffes and underpants. I was recently bought a Northern Soul kitchen apron as a present. People who were not born when the last of Northern Soul's great clubs closed show up at current clubs covered in badges recalling The Torch, Wigan Casino, The Pendulum and the rest. People refer to themselves and other aficionados as 'Soulies' and add 'K T F' (Keep the Faith) to the end of their messages. From being an incidental part of the scene, visible public statements of allegiance to Northern Soul have become central.

*Northern Soul bags on sale, Blackpool, 2012. Photo credit: Stephen Riley*

The black fist salute has an important history, symbolising the struggle of black Americans against the apartheid system then operating in several American states, and a more widespread, more subtle discrimination, which still persists. The Northern Soul scene appropriated the emblem, partly to express solidarity, but mostly to symbolise its commitment to black American music. A UK-based firm that makes Northern Soul memorabilia recently tried to copyright the black fist symbol, to make it its own, to prevent others from using it and thereby to make as much money out of it as possible. Common sense prevailed and they failed, but the attempt on the part of that firm to possess, for commercial gain, an emblem that originally represented the aspirations of an oppressed people and later a love of the music of those people on the part of British youth, is indicative of how distorted things have become. As if to mark the absurdities that occur when such marketing becomes so far detached from the source that created it, the black fist is often reproduced in white ink on a dark ground, so Northern Soul is no longer represented by a black fist but a white one. Similarly, an old Twisted Wheel logo, which featured the red rose of Lancashire, is also reproduced in white on a coloured ground, so the red rose becomes a white rose, and Lancashire is represented by its traditional enemy, Yorkshire. The fact that people buy this stuff without caring about the contradiction, or without it even registering, is indicative of how distanced the products and consumers have become from the original meaning of these symbols. It's rather like pulling on a Manchester City shirt to support Manchester United: near enough isn't it? They're both Manchester. Northern market halls proffer cheap, plastic Northern Soul shoulder bags, on which the fist is available in a range of colours: purple, blue, green… Perhaps the latter indicates that the wearer has a taste for music by Martians. My Northern Soul apron is dark blue with a yellow fist on it – possibly this means I am into singers with jaundice.

Many of those who were on the scene from before it went over ground object to all of this. In return, we are attacked for being 'elitist' or 'purist' or 'stuck in the past' or for being against any new people arriving on the scene. All of this misses the point. If we mouldy oldies take umbrage at being associated, against our will, with absurdities like those set out above (and below), I think we have a point.

So let's be clear: I do not know anyone who objects to new, young people coming to the clubs. Any fellow oldies who have expressed a view within my earshot have said that they like to see new, young people taking an interest, as it keeps the scene alive and re-affirms what we have always felt about the music. 'Elitism' makes no sense, either, because there is no 'elite'. The scene in its heyday was anarchic and driven by the people within it. Even if various people, clubs and records have been influential at various times, there never was a Northern Soul aristocracy, and there is no ideal club, piece of music or dancing style to be held up as an exemplar that could never be matched. Even Ian Levine – one of the scene's most significant figures – has been booed off stage for playing the wrong music (or maybe the right music, but to the wrong crowd). What a 'purist' might be is also dubious, as Northern Soul is a mongrel body of music, which incorporates Soul but many other related styles too. The situation is essentially the other way around: any Soul 'purist' would baulk at Northern Soul.

I should be clear, however, that new kinds of division have emerged – see section entitled 'Rarity, Divs and Handbaggers', above – but these are not based on new people coming to the scene, as such, but on irritation at those who grasp Northern Soul only by its clichés, who only want to listen to the scene's top twenty or so records, who trade in counterfeit copies of rare discs, who ill-use the scene by exploiting its images, or who don't understand the etiquette expected at Northern Soul clubs and make a nuisance of themselves.

I use the term 'cognoscenti' to describe those who feel and express that irritation, but this is not an 'elite'; it is just a broad group of people involved now or in the past with Northern Soul, who enjoy the music and the scene and who share a feeling of dismay at these aspects. The following anecdote from a spat going on, on Facebook, as I write, is indicative.

An individual – let's call him 'A' – placed on one of the various Northern Soul-related groups a photo of a selection of 'Northern Soul' beer towels. In their original guise – carrying a brewer's name and logo – these were commonplace on 1970s bar tops, to wipe-up spilt drinks; and they were sometimes nicked by Northern Soul aficionados, who would tuck them down their belts and use them to mop their sweat whilst dancing in hot, crowded all-nighters. The ones in the photo, however, have Northern Soul-related logos where the brewers' ones would once have been: the insignia of various clubs, the obligatory black fist and the usual exhortation to 'Keep the Faith'. Another individual – let's call him 'B' – on taking umbrage at this, cut and pasted the image onto his timeline in order to express his irritation and disdain, and countless of his Facebook friends joined in and commented disparagingly on this example of the scene's images being exploited. 'A' saw the post and the comments that had followed it, and expressed his outrage at the mockery, mostly in the form of insults directed at 'B' and his friends. 'B' is a well-known and well-respected character, who has been on the Soul/Rare Soul/Northern Soul scene since the late 1960s. Several of those who leapt to B's defence drew attention to A's profile: it featured photographs of him with a large number of Northern Soul badges on both his jackets and trousers, some of which made reference to some of the well-known clubs from Northern Soul's 1960-70s heyday. It also showed his date of birth: 1969. He could not, therefore, have been to any of the clubs his badges celebrated, and this begs the question of what these badges signify when worn by him. This anecdote overall highlights where tensions exist between the apparently mouldy oldies and others: 'A' would be welcome to come to the current clubs by that earlier generation, but what rankles with those who actually went to the original clubs is that he appears to be pretending that he did too, when he clearly did not; that he is celebrating trashy, exploitative artefacts that have attached themselves to the scene; and that in covering himself in so many badges he is parodying the scene and its fashions – all without the nous to understand that he is doing so. In fairness to 'A', however, he is part of a wider body of people who do this, so from his perspective – detached from the original scene – he is not parodying anything, he is subscribing to a badge-wearing, Northern Soul artefact-collecting fashion that came later. But then, to the cognoscenti, this is what makes him a div – he can't even see the faux pas he's engaged in.

In another similar social media exchange, someone had proudly posted a picture of his van, sprayed up with the words 'Northern Soul – Keep the Faith' on the sides. One of the wags who mocked it in the comments column pointed out that, back in the day, the last thing you would do was advertise that you had anything do with Northern Soul, as that would be a clear message to the Drug Squad that they would find what they were looking for in your vehicle. Again, the adorning of the van in this way betrays ignorance of the sub-cult being portrayed.

As for 'living in the past' – that is an ironic assertion, as it is often the contemporary appropriation of an imagined version of past dress codes etc. that oldies object to. The point being that, back in the day, the scene was fresh, vibrant and acutely fashion-conscious, with punters constantly on the lookout for the latest sound or style. The idea that the Northern Soul scene is characterised by some fixed, set-in-the-past look is the opposite of its original values. This paradoxical situation means that it is not unusual to see, at contemporary Northern Soul events, people too young to have ever been to any of the scene's 1970s clubs dressed in badge-covered 1973 baggies, standing next to authentic old Soul boys who wouldn't be seen dead in that stuff. Similarly, many of those who were around right at the start of Northern Soul scene bought new Soul sounds throughout the 70s and later, and continue to do so, whilst many younger devotees see Northern Soul as strictly 60s. Indeed, many 1970s records which were played on the Northern Soul scene when they were new – such as Crown Heights Affair's 'Dreaming a Dream', Sister Sledge's 'Love Don't Go Through No Changes on Me' and The Miracles' 'Love Machine' – are ignored and seem to have been written out of the revised history because they do not fit the 'it was all about 60s music' narrative, although, paradoxically, there is a blind-spot for some favoured 1970s records, which are allowed in. See separate section on this. It is not unreasonable for people who were around at the time to object to the history they lived through being inaccurately rewritten by people who were not there.

First time around, Northern Soul was a counter-culture. It was separated out from mainstream culture by being partly hidden from view, though anyone could join in if they wanted to. They would, however, have to endure the informal rites of initiation: feeling awkward at first amongst a knowledgeable and confident crowd of existing insiders, not understanding values and how things worked, wearing the wrong clothes and not being able to dance in the right way. The films *Soul Boy* (2010) and *Northern Soul* (2014) depict this process of initiation, following characters from embarrassing, gangly awkwardness through to expertise. The scene was also partly secret because of the rarity of the records and sometimes their being deliberately covered-up to retain their obscurity, but also because it lived with one foot in illegality, due to drug use and the associated acquisitional activities. Also, unless you were very lucky, the clubs were a long way away, and going to them involved a degree of effort, organisation, knowledge and commitment, unlike popping to the local disco. Some of the clubs were scruffy, ominous places, with bad reputations, which more nervous and maybe more sensible teenagers would avoid. Drug use, dealing, skinhead antics and seriousness about the music meant that these places differed from the 'get pissed, arse about on the dancefloor, chat up a girl' ethos of mainstream discos. All of this denotes a scene darker and more underground than the one now much imagined.

Northern Soul also, at first, used that classic oppositional strategy of appropriating capitalism's products and re-using them on its own terms. The makers and purveyors of the music that was played had no knowledge of the scene of which they had become part. Usually, chosen tracks had been failures first time around or even ignored B-sides and many had not been made available to a non-US audience. The scene also defined its own fashions. Northern Soul fans took their ideas to tailors and had clothes made to their own specifications. For a time, there was a kind of 'arms race' to get ever wider trousers with ever more pockets. These designs were later copied and mass produced. A personal anecdote from 1972 might be indicative. I decided I wanted a new Fred Perry-esque polo shirt to wear to the next Torch all-nighter. I could not afford a real Fred Perry, so I got an unbranded polo shirt, which cost about half the price, instead. Lacking the usual logo on the left side of the chest, it looked a bit plain, but something I'd seen at The Torch gave me an idea: a guy had been wearing a Simon-style, pin-tuck shirt with an embroidered badge depicting a man and woman in the '69' position, underscored by the words 'right on'. I had no desire to depict extracts from the Kama Sutra, so I went to my record collection for inspiration and found myself drawn to the logo on one of my 'Okeh' label records. I copied the word 'Okeh' in the style in which it was printed on the label onto the shirt in biro and got my mum to embroider over it in white cotton. It looked a treat: like a real, professional-looking logo, but depicting one of my favourite labels instead of Fred Perry's laurel wreath. When I went to The Torch, I was asked by two or three people where I had got the logo'd shirt from, and I told them the story. When I was next at The Torch, I saw someone with a polo shirt with an oval, fabric badge on the left side of the chest. The badge was purple, like the Okeh label, and had the word 'Okeh' embroidered onto it. Similarly, on my first trip to The Torch, dancing frenetically for most of the night, I found myself dripping with sweat. For my next visit, therefore, I showed up wearing a tennis-style wrist band to mop my brow with when I was dancing. I subsequently noticed lots of people wearing them. By the time Wigan Casino got going, they were a standard piece of Northern Soul regalia. I need to be abundantly clear, here, that I am not suggesting that I invented the Northern Soul badge or the wearing of sweat bands – people often generate similar ideas at the same time for the same reasons, plus, the use of cloth badges on blazers had been around on the scene for some time, and my polo-shirt idea was partly informed by the guy with the soixante-neuf badge, and the appropriation of sports gear and the decorating of parkas go back at least as far as the Mods – but this is indicative of the ways in which individual creativity and appropriation were intrinsic to Northern Soul. It was about doing it yourself, not waiting for someone to think it up in a focus group and dole it out from a factory.

Add to all this Northern Soul's oblique connection to the politics of resistance, through its nodding acquaintance with the black American Civil Rights Movement, and you have a clearly delineated scene that was conscious of, and took pleasure in, its outsider status.

All of this contrasts starkly with what happened from the mid-70s, when the scene went over ground and the media and commercial interests wrested influence away from the grass roots. The contrast to the present scene is even more glaring and, in effect, the values of the scene have been slammed into reverse. From being under-ground, the scene is very much now over-ground. Indeed, references to Northern Soul are hard to avoid, even cropping up in soft, establishment-stalwart settings like University Challenge. Far from being a counter-culture that appropriates capitalism's tokens in its own way, it is the recipient of its own tokens, re-appropriated and sold back by commercial interests. Far from being an anarchic, obscure, often illegal netherworld, it is now the object of sanitising narratives, which deny its past and remake it as a wholesome, brotherly/sisterly scene. Whereas the brands that were associated with Northern Soul in the early 70s were the likes of drug companies Riker and S,K&F, the scene is so wholesome now that it is used to advertise Shredded Wheat, playing on its health-giving qualities – the music and the product both being good for the heart, apparently. The effect of all of this is that Northern Soul has lost its edge and its freedom. It was free to operate anarchically, making its own choices of music, fashion, clubs, and values. Now, all of these things are fixed – shaped and fashioned in some invisible place, and re-presented back as what and how Northern Soul is. Again, those who were part of the original scene are, in my view, justified in lamenting its loss and its replacement with a top-down parody, and even, to a degree, to being a tad pissed-off with those who fall for the parody. Though, having said that, not everyone has a sociology degree, and cultural phenomena don't come with handbooks explaining their social significance and pitfalls, and few would be expected to view Northern Soul through concepts such as identity politics, cultural appropriation and recuperation, so there has to be forgiveness, and there usually is.

Each of Northern Soul's revivals has not been an exact copy of what went before, and in the manner of a Chinese whisper, it gets more distorted over time. The scene I arrived at in 69/70 was a reinvention of the Mod scene, but with faster records. The first reinvention of Northern Soul, the one from 1974/5 onwards, was characterised by exaggerations of most things. The baggy trousers most of us had worn a couple of years earlier, but had now discarded in favour of A-line flares, were back again, but with more flaps and buttons and sometimes badges. For some, shirts with multiple badges were now the in thing, when we antecedents were, by now, wearing fitted poly-cotton and cheesecloth shirts: the fashions of the day. What had been the odd backdrop and spin became the main event. Dancing wasn't just to be done, it was to be seen to be done and celebrated in competitions (and re-celebrated in anniversaries, and the anniversaries had then to be re-celebrated with commemorative badges). The moment in the film *Northern Soul*, when the protagonists react with amused dismay on hearing that this novel thing, a 'dance competition', has been held, captures the reaction of many at the time (the film narrative begins in 1974) to what were seen by many as asinine developments.

I feel the need to be very clear about what I am saying and what I am not saying in this. I am sure that many people who came to Northern Soul after 1974 were deeply involved in the scene and have an in-depth knowledge of the music, the clubs and the whole milieu. What is also clear, however, is that many who came did so because it was the latest fad; they then dipped their toes and left. And now, having never really immersed themselves in the scene, hold their thinly-supported opinions to be expert knowledge. I support this view by the numbers on social media whose favourite records are not Soul records at all, who believe the Northern Soul scene was a drug-free environment and who, by their ages, give away the fact that they weren't old enough to have been there at the time, or were just old enough to have caught the scene in its late-1970s decline, when it was already a loose-fitting parody of what had gone before. What has also been telling is the fierce response to the way the film *Northern Soul* focused on drugs, violence and the underground aspects of the scene. But, speaking as someone who was there, that is pretty much how it was. Indeed, the film was pretty mild, compared to the reality. Many involved lived on the margins. The drugs used were illegal; the activities required to get them were illegal; and the deals, rip-offs, drug-induced paranoid states, betrayals (real and imagined), encounters with the Law, overdoses, deaths, diseases and so on that were part of this meant that things could get very nasty indeed. There was an netherworld of criminal activity that went on around Northern Soul to support its pharmaceutical needs. And that's without thinking about the casual approach back then to driving: few paid much attention to what state they were in when they jumped behind the wheels of their Marinas, Avengers and Cortinas. One wag on Facebook likened the scene back then to the 'Wild West'. Horses aside, that is not a bad analogy. However, there is a body of opinion that either does not know about all of this or prefers to ignore it. Whatever the case, there is a large number of people who project a distorted, sanitised history onto Northern Soul.

Punk makes a useful analogy. You start with the fleeting brilliance of the Sex Pistols and the searing live performances of the Clash, and within no time you have Billy Idol sneering theatrically at the Top of the Pops cameras; the cringe-inducing Toyah Wilcox preaching as 'The High Priestess of Punk', when the noises she made sounded like its nemesis; and a Radio One DJ, who'd grown up in the leafy Home Counties, putting on a shmockney accent and singing in a punkish idiom about the miseries of an inner-city, high-rise life he'd never seen. The form had been understood and was easy to mimic. The moment of anarchy was over. Northern Soul had a longer innings – the late 60s to the mid-70s – but the experience of loss is equivalent.

What happened to the music itself was the biggest disaster – a real omnishambles. When the good burghers of Wigan Casino, with Pye and Spark record labels, took the Northern Soul scene over ground, the records at the forefront were largely their own, self-generated nightmares, such as 'Ski-ing in the Snow' and 'Footsee' and other non-Soul records. The combination of Wigan Casino's music policy and a huge influx of newcomers, who evidently did not have the musical discernment to reject this music, meant that the world at large came to know Northern Soul through an advert for a children's toy (Footsee) and Top of the Pops performances by the likes of Londoner, Wayne Gibson, and Lancastrian club-circuit band, Wigan's Ovation. For those already on the scene, who had cut their teeth on records by real Soul greats, like Otis Redding, Wilson Pickett and Aretha Franklin, this was effectively a public humiliation. We had been part of a cool, underground scene, which centred on the best that popular music had to offer. Not only had our scene been made public, which no-one particularly wanted, what had been made public was a perverse parody of it. Your mum, your dad, the people at work and everyone else now knew what Northern Soul sounded like, and it sounded like Wigan's Ovation, Wigan's Chosen Few and Nosmo King and the Javells. And that wasn't the end of it: in tandem with this travesty, there came the insistence that only old records were valid. This inevitably meant that a finite body of music was being pursued, meaning that the quality bar was set ever lower and that the scene would necessarily disappear up its own tweeter – at least in Wigan Casino and places which adopted its approach to music. And all of this fed into the perception of Northern Soul that has come down to us now – one which is built on the lie that the Wigan Casino version of Northern Soul equals the Northern Soul experience. That reading of the scene is one that tries to exclude 1970s music; it tries to tell me that I never danced to George Benson's 'Supership', Betty Wright's 'Where is the Love', The Crown Heights Affair's 'Foxy Lady' and many others of their kind at Northern Soul clubs. It also means that DJs at Northern Soul functions now dare not spin tracks like these for fear of clearing the dancefloor.

I do not think it is unreasonable for lovers of Soul music and people who were on the scene before 1974 to resent the way it was taken over and represented to the public with bad pop music; or to resent the way the scene was fixed into the past, ensuring its demise; or to object a perverse history of the scene, which insists that some of music we listened to was not part of the scene and has to be re-filed under headings such as 'disco', 'jazz-funk' or 'modern', when all of it was played at the time in Northern Soul clubs.

Objection on the part of the Mouldy Oldies is not, therefore, what it appears to be: it is not just meanness, elitism or a desire to pull up the drawbridge before any further new people can get in. The objection is to the scene's recuperation, commercialisation and its reduction to a set of simplistic and often wrong stereotypes; it is to a dishonest re-imagining of the scene, by some, as an idealised, drug-free, violence-free, utopian place of brotherly and sisterly love; it is to having the scene handed (or sold) back as a misshapen parody; it is to having music we listened to rendered retrospectively invalid and ejected from the scene; it is to having the fashions we wore reinvented and styles that don't conform to the redrafted history excluded; it is to being told by people who were not there that what we lived through and what we remember never happened; it is to having friends who were killed by drug use implicitly erased from the history of the scene because they do not fit the preferred narrative; it is to having our own personal histories invalidated and reinvented.

Even then, it must be stressed that no-one can stop the scene evolving and new people pulling it into the shape that suits them. Recuperation happens and could not have been stopped. That inevitability, however, is not a reason to accept a reinvented version of the scene's history, and in my view it is important for all of those who were there and are honest to stand up and tell the truth.

# Conclusion

There will be those who, on reading this, might think I dislike Northern Soul. After all, many of the things I have said are not complimentary and do not endeavour to show the scene in the best possible light. But I think only those who have read it in a superficial way will think that. The truth is I love Northern Soul – the music and the scene – and have done so since the first time I encountered it. I still listen to it regularly to this day and always will, and I still attend Northern Soul clubs and I remain in touch with other life-long and new Northern Soul fans.

This book has not been about undermining Northern Soul, just telling the truth as I lived it, and if that is sometimes a bit uncomfortable, well so be it. As they say: a friend will tell you what you want to hear; a real friend will tell you what you need to hear. I hope I am a real friend to Northern Soul.

It is often said that we are all middle class now. To my mind that is a myth and one of many means of keeping us from seeing the real state of our lives, but some of us have made some kind of upward social transition and many of us see ourselves has having done so, even if the criteria by which we measure that shift are dubious. But, whatever the case, we now live in the post-buy-your-own-council-house and post-political-correctness era. Values have changed radically since the 1970s, and whether we are middle class or not, our moral compasses have been reprogrammed, because of these changing social values and because of our own maturity. Forty-odd years ago, we might have found ourselves worrying where the drugs for next weekend's all-nighter were coming from; now we're worried whether our kids (or grandkids) are taking them. Even the legal stuff is now met with reproach: smoking is a no-no and we are taught to be anxious about how many units of alcohol we consume. And we've switched sides in the 'us and them' dichotomy: by now, many of us will be the supervisor, rather than the shop-floor guy; and most of will align ourselves with the police and their role in the community, when back in the day they were, at best, to be avoided, at worst, the enemy.

We are not the people we were when we were first on the scene and we do not have the same values, and it is not honest to reinvent the past on the basis of a new, more mature and ethically-modified view of the world. And many, of course, refuse to do so – I hope you ladies and gentlemen appreciate this book in all its candour. But there remains a body of opinion that wants to sweeten Northern Soul's past to make it fit contemporary values. It is against that body of opinion that this book addresses itself, and I hope I have provided ample evidence to make my case.

The Northern Soul scene in its heyday was peopled by youth, with all the wildness and recklessness that implies. We made the scene, we were the scene, and we didn't mind the drugs and the fighting and the bootlegged records; in fact many of us rather liked them – they were part of the excitement – and as uncomfortable as that may seem now, it is the truth.

# Sources

- A Clockwork Orange (1971) Film. Dir. Stanley Kubrick
- BBC Living for the Weekend (2014) [online] Available on YouTube: https://www.youtube.com/watch?v=_jHx4AoCk4k [Accessed 11 January 2018]
- Billy Elliot. (2000) Film. Dir. Stephen Daldry
- Bullock, A., Stallybrass, O., Trombley, S. The Fontana Dictionary of Modern Thought. Fontana, London. 1988
- Dictionary.com [online] Available: http://www.dictionary.com/browse/genre [Accessed 23 November 2014]
- Greer, Germaine. The Female Eunuch (1970) Edition: Harper Perennial Classics, New York. 2006
- Hardman, Isabel. 26 Sept. 2013. Tories are searching for their Northern Soul. The Telegraph [online] Available: http://www.telegraph.co.uk/news/politics/conservative/10336844/Tories-are-searching-for-their-northern-Soul.html [Accessed 29 May 2016]
- Hinkley Soul Club [online] Available: http://rareSoul.org.uk/hinckley-Soulclub/wheel.htm [Accessed 25 January 2017]
- Martinsbox.tripod.com Jeff Kings (sic) Thing [online] Available: http://martinsbox.tripod.com/id60.htm [Accessed 28 May 2016]
- Mason, Paul 23 Sept. 2013 Poor-Man's Speed: Coming of Age in Wigan's Anarchic Northern Soul Scene [online] Available: http://www.vice.com/en_uk/read/northern-Soul-revival-wigan-casino-paul-mason [Accessed 23 May 2016]
- Northern Soul. (2014) Film. Dir. Elaine Constantine
- Nuttall, Jeff. Bomb Culture. McGibbon and Key, London. 1968
- Quadrophenia. (1979) Film, Dir. Franc Roddam
- Slaughter and the Dogs. 1977 Where Have All the Boot Boys Gone (music and video) [online] Available https://www.youtube.com/watch?v=dILXRY8JiKg [online] [Accessed 19 April 2017]
- Soul Boy. (2010) Film. Dir. Shimmy Marcus

- Soul Source [online] Available: https://www.soul-source.co.uk/ [Accessed 26 February 2018]
- Thomas, Ceri. 6 October 2015. What's the truth about the VIP 'paedophile ring'? BBC News Online Magazine [online] Available http://www.bbc.co.uk/news/magazine-34442292 [Accessed 20 September 2017]
- Trainspotting (1996) Film. Dir. Danny Boyle
- The Twisted Wheel [online] Available: http://www.twistedwheel.com/page13.html [Accessed 8 December 2014]
- Warburton, Nick. Vanda and Young post-Easybeats: Paintbox, Moondance and Tramp. Garagehangover [online] Available: http://www.garagehangover.com/vandaandyoung/ [Accessed 23 June 2016]
- Wikipedia [online] Twisted Wheel Club Available: https://en.wikipedia.org/wiki/Twisted_Wheel_Club [Accessed 9 January 2018]
- Wikipedia [online] Norman Wisdom Available: https://en.wikipedia.org/wiki/Norman_Wisdom [Accessed 3 June 2016]
- Wilson, Tony. 24 Hour Party People. Pan MacMillan, London, 2002

# Discography

This is a list of records mentioned or alluded to in this book. Please note: these are not all Northern Soul records. Many are by no means recommended listening, but are there for completeness because they got a mention. Indeed, some are included only to illustrate how awful or out of place they are. Their context can be found in the main body of the book.

Where this list appears in the Kindle edition of this book, there are links that will take the reader to ITunes where a small portion of that track can be listened to. The reader can also purchase that track via the ITunes portal.

100 Proof Aged in Soul – Somebody's Been Sleeping
Al 'TNT' Braggs – Earthquake
Al de Lory and Mandango – Right On
Al Greene and the Soul Mates – Don't Leave Me
Al Hudson and the Soul Partners – Spread Love
Al Kent – Ooh Pretty Lady
Al Kent – You've Got to Pay the Price
Al Wilson – The Snake
Alexander Patton – A Lil' Lovin' Sometimes
Alvin Cash and The Registers – Philly Freeze
Alvin Cash and The Crawlers – Twine Time
Andre Brasseur – The Kid
Arthur Conley – Funky Street
Arthur Conley – Sweet Soul Music
August and Deneen – We Go Together
Babe Ruth – Elusive
Barbara Acklin – Am I the Same Girl
Barbara Acklin – Love Makes a Woman
Barbara and Brenda – Never Love a Robin
Barbara Lewis – Someday We're Gonna Love Again
Barbara Randolph – I Got a Feeling

Barnaby Bye – Can't Live This Way
Beau Dollar and The Coins – Soul Serenade
Ben Zine – Village of Tears
Bessie Banks – I Can't Make It (Without You baby)
Betty Everett – Getting Mighty Crowded
Betty Everett – It's in His Kiss
Betty Wright – Where is the Love
Beverley Ann – He's Coming Home
Beverley Ann – You've Got Your Mind On Other Things
Bill Brandon and Lorraine Johnson – Let Me Be Your Full Time Groover
Bill Cosby – Little Ole Man (Uptight – Everything's Alright)
Bill Harris – Uptown Saturday Night
Bill Moss – Sock it to 'Em Soul Brother
Billy Butler – The Right Track
Billy Davis – Three Steps From True Love
Billy Preston – Billy's Bag
Billy Ocean – Love Really Hurts Without You
Billy Woods – Let Me Make You Happy
Black Nasty – Cut Your Motor Off
Blanch Carter – Halos are for Angels
Bob and Earl – Harlem Shuffle
Bob Brady and the ConChords – Everybody's Going to a Love In
Bob Brady and the ConChords – More More More of Your Love
Bob Kuban and the In Men – The Cheater
Bob Wilson and the San Remo Strings – All Turned On
Bobbi Lynn – Earthquake
Bobby Bland – Call on Me
Bobby Bland – Shoes
Bobby Goldsboro – Honey
Bobby Goldsboro – It's Too Late
Bobby Goldsboro – Too Many People
Bobby Hebb – Love Love Love
Bobby Hutton – Lend a Hand
Bobby Jason – Wall to Wall Heartaches
Bobby Paris – I Walked Away
Bobby Paris – Night Owl
Bobby Paris – Per-so-nal-ly
Bobby Sheen – Dr. Love
Bobby Wells – Let's Copp a Groove
Boby Franklin – The Ladies Choice
Booker T and the MGs – Green Onions
Booker T and the MGs – Time is Tight
Boris Gardner – Elizabethan Reggae

Brenda and the Tabulations – A Love You Can Depend On
Brian Hyland – The Joker Went Wild
Brooks and Jerry – I Got What It Takes
Bud Harper – Mr. Soul
Bunny Sigler – Let the Good Times Roll and Feel So Good
Candy and the Kisses – The 81
Carl Douglas – Kung Fu Fighting
Chairmen of the Board – Everything's Tuesday
Chairmen of the Board – Give Me Just a Little More Time
Chairmen of the Board – You've Got Me Dangling on a String
Chapter Five – You Can't Mean It
Charles Wright – Keep Saying (You Don't Love Nobody)
Charlie Gracie – He'll Never Love You Like I Do
Charlie Rich – Love is After Me
Chris Montez – Let's Dance
Chubby Checker – At the Discotheque
Chubby Checker – Everything's Wrong
Chuck Jackson – Chains of Love
Chuck Jackson – Good Things Come to Those Who Wait
Chuck Jackson – I've Got the Need
Chuck Wood – Seven Days Too Long
Clara Ward – The Right Direction
Cliff Nobles and Co. – The Horse
Clifford Curry – I Can't Get a Hold of Myself
Cobblestone – Trick Me, Treat Me
Connie Laverne – Can't Live Without You Baby
Creation – I Got the Fever
Curtis Mayfield – Move On Up
Dandy – Reggae in Your Jeggae
Darrell Banks – Open the Door to Your Heart
Darrell Banks – Our Love is in the Pocket
Darrow Fletcher – Gotta Draw the Line
David and the Giants – Superlove
David and the Giants – Ten Miles High
Dean Parrish – Determination
Dean Parrish – I'm on My Way
Dean Parrish – Tell Her
Debbie Fleming – Long Gone
Derek and Ray – Interplay
Desmond Dekker – It Mek
Desmond Dekker – The Israelites
Diana Ross and the Supremes – There's No Stopping Us Now
Dionne Warwick – Anyone Who Had a Heart

Dionne Warwick – There's Always Something There to Remind Me
Dobie Gray – Out on the Floor
Dobie Gray – The In Crowd
Don Covay and the Goodtimers – See Saw
Don Downing – Dreamworld
Don Ray – Born a Loser
Don Thomas – Come on Train
Donald Height – Talk of the Grapevine
Donnie Elbert – Little Piece of Leather (1965 version)
Dooley Silverspoon – Game Players
Doris Day – Move Over Darling
Doris Troy – I'll Do Anything
Doris Troy – Just One Look
Dusty Springfield – What's It Gonna Be
Earl Harrison – Humphrey Stomp
Earl Jean – I'm into Something Good
Earl van Dyke and the Motown Brass – 6 by 6
Earl van Dyke and the Soul Brothers – I Can't Help Myself (Sugar Pie, Honey Bunch)
Earl van Dyke and the Soul Brothers Orchestra – All for You
Earth Wind and Fire – Happy Feeling
East Coast Connection – Summer in the Parks
Eddie Floyd – Bring it on Home to Me
Eddie Floyd – Don't Tell Your Mama
Eddie Floyd – Things Get Better
Eddie Holland – Candy to Me
Eddie Kendricks – Keep on Truckin'
Eddie Parker – Love You Baby
Eddie Regan – Playing Hide and Seek
Edwin Starr – Agent Double-O-Soul
Edwin Starr – Back Street
Edwin Starr – Headline News
Edwin Starr – I Want My Baby Back
Edwin Starr – My Weakness is You
Edwin Starr – Stop Her on Sight (SOS)
Edwin Starr – Time
Edwin Starr – War
Edwin Starr – Way Over There
Edwin Starr – Twenty Five Miles
Eighth Avenue Band – Whole Thing
Eloise Laws – Love Factory
Elvis Presley – Mystery Train
Elvis Presley – Rubberneckin'

Errol Dixon – I Want
Esther Phillips – What a Difference a Day Makes
Eula Cooper – Let Our Love Grow Higher
Evie Sands – Picture Me Gone
Fantastic Johnny C – Don't Depend On Me
Felice Taylor – I Feel Love Comin' On
First Choice – Armed and Extremely Dangerous
First Choice – This is the House Where Love Died
Fontella Bass – Recovery
Fontella Bass – Rescue Me
Frances Nero – Keep on Loving Me
Frank Wilson – Do I love You (Indeed I Do)
Frankie (Love Man) Crocker – Ton of Dynamite
Frankie and Johnny – I'll Hold You
Frankie Valli – You're Ready Now
Frankie Valli and the Four Seasons – I'm Gonna Change
Frankie Valli and the Four Seasons – The Night
Freda Payne – Band of Gold
Freda Payne – Deeper and Deeper
Freda Payne – Rock Me in the Cradle (of Your Lovin' Arms)
Garland Green – Sending My Best Wishes
Gary Lewis and the Playboys – My Heart's Symphony
Gene Chandler – Nothing Can Stop Me
Gene Chandler – There Was a Time
Gene Chandler and Barbara Acklin – From the Teacher to the Preacher
Gene Latter – Sign on the Dotted Line
George Benson – Love Ballad
George Benson – Supership
George Torrence – Lickin' Stick
Gil Scott Heron – The Bottle
Gladys Knight and the Pips – Friendship Train
Gladys Knight and the Pips – Just Walk in My Shoes
Gloria Jones – Tainted Love
Gloria Taylor – You've Got to Pay the Price
Graham Central Station – Feel the Need in Me
Harold Melvin and the Blue Notes – Don't Leave Me This Way
Harry J All Stars – Liquidator
Hawaii Five-O – The Ventures
Helen Shapiro – Stop and You Will Become Aware
Herman's Hermits – I'm into Something Good
Hoagy Lands – Next in Line
Holly St James – That's Not Love
Homer Banks – 60 Minutes of Your Love

Homer Banks – Hooked by Love
Idris Muhammad – Could Heaven Ever Be Like This
Ike and Tina Turner – Crazy 'Bout You Baby
Ike and Tina Turner – Dust My Broom
Ila Vann – You Made Me This Way
Inez and Charlie Foxx – Tightrope
Isaac Hayes – Disco Connection
J J Barnes – Please Let Me In
J J Barnes – Real Humdinger
J J Jackson – But it's Alright
J J Jackson – Sho Nuff Got a Good Thing
Jackie Edwards – I Feel So Bad
Jackie Lee – Darkest Days
Jackie Lee – Do the Temptation Walk
Jackie Lee – Oh My Darling
Jackie Lee – Shotgun and the Duck
Jackie Lee – The Duck
Jackie Wilson – Higher and Higher
Jackie Wilson – I Get the Sweetest Feeling
Jackie Wilson – The Who Who Song
James and Bobby Purify – Do Unto Me
James and Bobby Purify – Let Love Come Between Us
James and Bobby Purify – Shake a Tail Feather
James Barnett – Keep on Talking
James Bounty – Prove Yourself a Lady
James Brown – Get Up I Feel Like Being a Sex Machine
James Brown – Hey America
James Brown - Living in America
James Brown – There Was a Time
James Brown and the Famous Flames – Papa's Got a Brand New Bag
James Carr – Freedom Train
James Carr – That's What I Want to Know
James Fountain – Seven Day Lover
James Lewis and The Case of Time – Manifesto
Jamo Thomas and His Party Brothers Orchestra – I Spy for the FBI
Jay and the Techniques – Apples Peaches Pumpkin Pie
Jay and the Techniques – Baby Make Your Own Sweet Music
Jay D Martin – By Yourself
Jay Traynor – Up and Over
Jerry Butler – Moody Woman
Jerry 'O' – Karate Boogaloo
Jimmy Breedlove – I Can't Help Loving You
Jimmy Cliff – Vietnam

Jimmy Conwell – Cigarette Ashes
Jimmy Holiday and Clydie King – Ready, Willing and Able
Jimmy Jackson and the Kantlose Orchestra – Footsteps in the Shadows
Jimmy Ruffin – I'll Say Forever My Love
Jimmy Ruffin – I've Passed This Way Before
Jimmy Ruffin – What Becomes of the Brokenhearted
Jo Armstead – I Feel an Urge Coming On
Joanie Summers – Don't Pity Me
Jobell and the Orchestra de Salsa – Never Gonna Let You Go
Jodi Mathis – Don't You Care Anymore
Joe Tex – Show Me
Joey Dee and the Starlighters – How Can I Forget
John E Paul – I Wanna Know
John Miles – Why Don't You Love Me
Johnny Sayles – I Can't Get Enough
Johnnie Taylor – Friday Night
Johnnie Taylor – Who's Making Love
Johnny Wyatt – This Thing Called Love
Judy Clay and William Bell – Private Number
Judy Harris – You Touched Me
Judy Street – What
Julien Covey and The Machine – A Little Bit Hurt
Junior Walker and the All Stars – Cleo's Back
Junior Walker and the All Stars – Cleo's Mood
Junior Walker and the All Stars – How Sweet It Is (To Be Loved by You)
Junior Walker and the All Stars – Roadrunner
Junior Walker and the All Stars – Shake and Fingerpop
Junior Walker and the All Stars – Shotgun
Junior Walker and the All Stars – What Does it Take
K C and the Sunshine Band – That's the Way I Like It
Karen Young – Too Much of a Good Thing
Kasenetz-Katz Singing Orchestral Circus – Quick Joey Small
Keith – Daylight Savin Time
Kelly Garrett – Love's the Only Answer
Kenny Smith – Lord, What's Happening to Your People
Kim Tolliver – I Don't Know What Foot to Dance On
Kim Weston – Helpless
Ko Ko Taylor – Wang Dang Doodle
Kool and the Gang – Kool and the Gang
Lada Edmund Jnr. – The Larue
Larry Santos – You Got Me Where You Want Me
Larry Saunders – On the Real Side
Larry Williams and Johnny Watson – A Quitter Never Wins

Larry Williams and Johnny Watson – Too Late
Laura Lee – To Win Your Heart
Len Barry – 1,2,3
Len Barry – Like a Baby
Leon Haywood – Baby Reconsider
Leroy Hutson – Ella Weez
Lesley Gore – We know We're in Love
Lester Tipton – This Won't Change
Life – Tell Me Why
Limmie and Family Cookin' – You Can Do Magic
Linda Jones – My Heart Needs a Break
Linda Jones and the Whatnauts – I'm So Glad I Found You
Linda Lyndell – Bring Your Love Back to Me
Little Anthony and the Imperials – Gonna Fix You Good
Little Carl Carlton – Competition Ain't Nothin'
Little Eva – The Locomotion
Little Hank – Mr Bang Bang Man
Little Mac and the Boss Sounds – In the Midnight Hour
Little Richard – A Little Bit of Something (Beats a Whole Lot of Nothing)
Little Richard – I Don't Want to Discuss It
Little Richard – Poor Dog (Who Can't Wag His Own Tail)
Lorraine Silver – Lost Summer Love
Los Canarios – Get on Your Knees
Lou Edwards and Today's People – Talkin' 'Bout Poor Folk
Lou Pride – I'm Com'un Home in the Morn'un
Lou Roberts and the Marks – Ten to One
Lou Roberts and the Marks – You Fooled Me
Lulu – Shout
Magic Disco Machine – Control Tower
Major Lance – Ain't No Soul (Left in These Old Shoes)
Major Lance – Monkey Time
Major Lance – The Beat
Major Lance – The Matador
Major Lance – Um Um Um Um Um
Major Lance – You Don't Want Me No More
Mandrill – Never Die
Margie Hendrix – Restless
Margo Thunder – The Soul of a Woman
Marlena Shaw – Let's Wade in the Water
Martha Reeves and the Vandellas – Dancing in the Street
Martha Reeves and the Vandellas – I Gotta Let You Go
Martha Reeves and the Vandellas – Jimmy Mack
Martha Reeves and the Vandellas – Nowhere to Run

Martha Reeves and the Vandellas – Third Finger Left Hand
Marv Johnson – I Miss You Baby (How I Miss You)
Marvin Gaye – I Heard it Through the Grapevine
Marvin Gaye – Little Darling (I Need You)
Marvin Gaye – Too Busy Thinking About My Baby
Marvin Gaye – Wherever I Lay My Hat
Marvin Gaye and Kim Weston – It Takes Two
Marvin Gaye and Tammi Terrell – The Onion Song
Marvin Gaye and Tammi Terrell – Two Can Have a Party
Marvin Holmes and Justice – You Better Keep Her
Mary Love – Lay This Burden Down
Mary Love – You Turned My Bitter Into Sweet
Mary Wells – My Guy
Mary Wells – What's Easy for Two is So Hard for One
Max Romeo – Wet Dream
Mel and Tim – Backfield in Motion
Mel Torme – Comin' Home Baby
Michael and Raymond – Man Without a Woman
Mickey Lee Lane – Hey Sa Lo Ney
Mickey Moonshine – Name It You Got It
Millie Jackson – A House for Sale
Millie Jackson – My Man a Sweet Man
Miriam Makeba – Pata Pata
Mistura featuring Lloyd Michels – The Flasher
Mitch Ryder and the Detroit Wheels – Break Out
Mitch Ryder and the Detroit Wheels – Devil With a Blue Dress / Good Golly Miss Molly
Mitch Ryder and the Detroit Wheels – You Get Your Kicks
Moment of Truth – Helplessly
Moses and Joshua – Get Out of My Heart
Moses and Joshua – My Illusive Dreams
Mr Bloe – Groovin with Mr Bloe
Mr Flood's Party – Compared to What
Muriel Day – Nine Time Out of Ten
Nancy Ames – I Don't Want to Talk About It
Nancy Wilson – The End of Our Love
Newby and Johnson – Sweet Happiness
Norman Greenbaum – Spirit in the Sky
Norman Johnson and the Showmen – Our Love Will Grow
Norman Wisdom – The Joker
Nosmo King and The Javells – Goodbye Nothing to Say
Oscar Perry and the Love Generators – I've Got What You Need
Otis Redding – Hard to Handle

Otis Redding – I Can't Turn You Loose
Otis Redding – I've Been Loving You Too Long
Otis Redding – Love Man
Otis Redding – Respect
Otis Redding – Satisfaction
Otis Redding – Shake
Otis Redding – Sitting on the Dock of the Bay
P J Proby – Nikki Hoeky
Pacific Gas and Electric – Are You Ready
Paintbox – Get Ready for Love
Pat Williams Orchestra – Theme from Police Story
Patti and the Emblems – I'm Gonna Love You a Long Long Time
Paul Anka – Can't Help Loving You
Paul Anka – When We Get There
Paul Humphrey – Cochise
Paul Kelly – Chills and Fever
Peaches and Herb – We're in this Thing Together
Peggy March – If You Loved Me
Percy Sledge – Baby Help Me
Phillip Mitchell – Free for All
Phyllis Hyman – You Know How to Love Me
Pierre Hunt – I've Got to Have Your Love
Prince Buster – Al Capone
Prince Buster – Ten Commandments of Man
Prince Buster – Wreck a Pum Pum
Prince George – Wrong Crowd
Prince Johnny Robinson – That Girl is Rated X
R B Freeman – I'm Shaft (You Ain't Shaft)
R Dean Taylor – There's a Ghost in My House
Rain – Out of My Mind
The Righteous Brothers Band – Rat Race
Raw Soul – The Gig
Reperata and the Delrons – It's Waiting There for You
Reperata and the Delrons – Panic
Rex Garvin and the Mighty Cravers – Sock It to 'em JB
Richard Temple – That Beatin' Rhythm
Robert Knight – Love on a Mountain Top
Robert Parker – Barefootin'
Robert Parker – Let's Go Baby (Where the Action is)
Roger Collins – She's Looking Good
Roger Collins –You Sexy Sugar Plum (But I Like It)
Roland Alphonso – Phoenix City
Rolf Harris – Two Little Boys

Ronnie Milsap – Ain't No Soul (Left in These Old Shoes)
Ronnie Walker – You've Got to Try Harder
Roscoe Robinson – That's Enough
Rosey Jones – Have Love Will Travel
Round Robin – Kick That Little Foot Sally Ann
Roy C – Shotgun Wedding
Roy Docker with Music Through Six – Mellow Moonlight
Roy Head – Treat Her Right
Sam and Dave – Hold on I'm Coming
Sam and Dave – I Thank You
Sam and Dave – Soothe Me
Sam and Dave – Soul Man
Sam and Dave – Soul Sister Brown Sugar
Sam and Dave – You Don't Know Like I know
Sam and Kitty – I've Got Something Good
Sam Cooke – Another Saturday Night
Sam Cooke – Twisting the Night Away
Sam the Sham and the Pharaohs – Ring Dang Doo
Sam the Sham and the Pharaohs – Woolly Bully
Sandi Sheldon – You're Gonna Make Me Love You
Sandra Phillips – World Without Sunshine
Shane Martin – I Need You
Shawn Elliott – The Joker
Sheila Anthony – Livin' in Love
Shirley Ellis – Soul Time
Shirley Ellis – The Clapping Song
Silvetti – Spring Rain
Sister Sledge – Love Don't You Go Through No Changes on Me
Sisters Love – I'm Learning to Trust My Man
Slaughter and the Dogs – Where Have All the Boot Boys Gone?
Sly and the Family Stone – Dance to the Music
Smokey Robinson and the Miracles – I Second that Emotion
Smokey Robinson and the Miracles – Tears of a Clown
Smokey Robinson and the Miracles – The Tracks of My Tears
Solomon King – This Beautiful Day
Sonny Charles and the Checkmates Ltd – Black Pearl
Sonny Stitt – Wade in the Water
Soul Brothers – Six Some Kind of Wonderful
Spooky & Sue – I've Got the Need
Steam – Na Na Hey Hey Kiss Him Goodbye
Stemmons Express – Woman, Lover Thief
Stevie Wonder – I Was Made to Love Her
Stevie Wonder – Uptight

Sue Lynne – Don't Pity Me
Sugar Pie DeSanto – Soulful Dress
Susan Barrett – What's It Gonna be
Sweet Sensation – Sad Sweet Dreamer
Symarip – Skinhead Moonstomp
Tami Lynn – I'm Gonna Run Away From You
Tavares - Heaven Must Be Missing an Angel
Tavares – It Only Takes a Minute
The Ad Libs – Nothing Worse than Being Alone
The Ad-Libs – The Boy from New York City
The Allnight Band – The Wigan Joker
The Amboy Dukes – Who's Fooling Who
The Anderson Brothers – I Can See Him Loving You
The Angels – My Boyfriend's Back
The Artistics – Hope We Have
The Artistics – I'm Gonna Miss You
The Astors – Candy
The Baltimore and Ohio Marching Band – Condition Red
The Bar-Kays – Sang and Dance
The Bar-Kays – Soul Finger
The Biddu Orchestra – Exodus
The Biddu Orchestra – Northern Dancer
The Blendells – Dance With Me
The Blendells – La La La La La
The Boogie Man Orchestra – Lady Lady Lady
The Brothers – Are You Ready for This
The Burning Bush – Keeps on Burning
The Cameo Players (aka Cameo) – Find My Way
The Capitols – Ain't that Terrible
The Carrolls – We're in this Thing Together
The Carstairs – It Really Hurts Me Girl
The Castaways – Liar Liar
The Chambers Brothers – I Can't Turn You Loose
The Cherry People – And Suddenly
The Chiffons – Keep the Boy Happy
The Chiffons – Out of this World
The Chiffons – Sweet Talking Guy
The Commodore – The Zoo (The Human Zoo)
The Contours – First I Look at the Purse
The Contours – It's So Hard Being a Loser
The Contours – Just a Little Misunderstanding
The Crow – Your Autumn of Tomorrow
The Crown Heights Affair – Dreaming a Dream

The Crown Heights Affair – Foxy Lady
The Crusaders – Put It Where you Want It
The Crystals – Da Doo Ron Ron
The Detroit Spinners – I'll Always Love You
The Dixie Cups – Chapel of Love
The Drifters – At the Club
The Drifters – Baby What I Mean
The Drifters – Saturday Night at the Movies
The Drifters – Sweets for my Sweet
The Drifters – Under the Boardwalk
The Drifters – You Got to Pay Your Dues
The Dynatones – Fife Piper
The Elgins – Heaven Must Have Sent You
The Elgins – Put Yourself in My Place
The Equals – Black Skin Blue Eyed Boys
The Esko Affair – Salt and Pepper
The Esquires – And Get Away
The Esquires – Get on Up
The Fabulous Counts – Lunar Funk
The Fascinations – Girls are Out to Get You
The Five Stairsteps and Cubie – Stay Close to Me
The Flaming Ember – Westbound Number Nine
The Flamingos – Boogaloo Party
The Flirtations – Nothing But a Heartache
The Flower Shoppe – You've Come a Long Way Baby
The Formations – At the Top of the Stairs
The Four Seasons – Opus 17(Don't You Worry About Me)
The Four Seasons – Sherry
The Four Seasons – Working My Way Back to You
The Four Tops – I Can't Help Myself
The Four Tops – Reach Out I'll be There
The Four Tops – Shake Me Wake Me
The Four Tops – Since You've Been Gone
The Four Tops – Something About You
The Four Tops – Standing in the Shadows of Love
The Four Tops – Without the One You Love
The Generation – Hold On
The Goodies – Black Pudding Bertha (The Queen of Northern Soul)
The Holidays – Makin' Up Time
The Hollies – Just One Look
The Honey Cone – While You're Out Looking for Sugar
The Human Beinz – Nobody But Me
The Impressions – Amen

The Impressions – I Can't Satisfy
The Impressions – You've Been Cheating
The Incredibles – There's Nothing Else to Say
The Intruders – I'll Always Love My Mama
The Invitations – Skiing in the Snow
The Invitations – What's Wrong with Me Baby
The Isley Brothers – Behind a Painted Smile
The Isley Brothers – I Guess I'll Always Love You
The Isley Brothers – I've Got a Feeling
The Isley Brothers – Put Yourself in My Place
The Isley Brothers – Shout
The Leon Young Strings – Glad All Over (Instrumental)
The Magic Night – If You and I Had Never Met
The Mar-Keys – Last Night
The Marvelettes – Please Mr Postman
The Marvelettes – Reaching for Something I Can't Have
The Marvelettes – When You're Young and in Love
The McCoys – Hang on Sloopy
The Mike Cotton Sound – Soul Serenade
The Miracles – Love Machine
The Miracles – That's What Love is Made Of
The Miracles – You Really Got a Hold on Me
The Moments – I've Got the Need
The Moments – Nine Times
The Moments – Sweet Sweet Lady
The Montclairs – Hung Up on Your Love
The Mood Mosaic – A Touch of Velvet - A Sting of Brass
The Natural Four – The Devil Made Me Do It
The Newbeats – Bread and Butter
The Newbeats – Don't Turn Me Loose
The Newbeats – Run Baby Run
The Nite-Liters – K-Jee
The O'Jays – 992 Arguments
The O'Jays – Backstabbers
The O'Jays – Deeper (In Love With You)
The O'Jays – I Love Music
The O'Jays – Lipstick Traces (On a Cigarette)
The O'Jays – Looky Looky (At Me Girl)
The O'Jays – Love Train
The O'Jays – Working on Your Case
The O'Kaysions – Girl Watcher
The Olympics – Baby Do the Philly Dog
The Olympics – Mine Exclusively

The Olympics – Same Old Thing
The Packers – Go Head On
The Packers – Hole in the Wall
The Pallbearers – Music with Soul
The Platters – Sweet Sweet Loving
The Platters – Washed Ashore
The Platters – With this Ring
The Poets – She Blew a Good Thing
The Pointer Sisters – Send Him Back
The Prophets – I Got the Fever
The Quadraphonics – Bet You If You Check It Out
The Radiants – Hold On
The Ramsey Lewis Trio – Wade in the Water
The Reflections – Like Adam and Eve
The Reflections – Three Steps From True Love
The Rimshots – Do What You Feel
The Ron Grainger Orchestra – Theme from Joe 90
The Ronettes – (The Best Part of) Breakin' Up
The Ronettes – Be My Baby
The San Remo Strings – Festival Time
The Sapphires – Gotta Have Your Love
The Searchers – Sweets for My Sweet
The Shades of Blue – Oh How Happy
The Shakers – One Wonderful Moment
The Sharonettes – Papa Ooh Mow Mow
The Short Kuts featuring Eddie Harrison – Your Eyes May Shine
The Showstoppers – Ain't Nothing but a House Party
The Skatalites – Guns of Navarone
The Skullsnaps – I'm Your Pimp
The Skullsnaps – My Hang-Up is You
The Soul Sisters – Good Time Tonight
The Soul Sisters – Wreck a Buddy
The Spellbinders – Chain Reaction
The Spellbinders – Help Me
The Spencer Davis Group – Trampoline
The Stylistics – I Can't Give You Anything (But My Love)
The Supremes – Baby Love
The Supremes – Where Did Our Love Go
The Tams – Be Young Be Foolish Be Happy
The Tams – Hey Girl Don't Bother Me
The Tams – Silly Little Girl
The Temptations – Ain't Too Proud to Beg
The Temptations – Beauty's Only Skin Deep

The Temptations – Cloud Nine
The Temptations – Get Ready
The Temptations – Girl, Why You Wanna Make Me Blue
The Temptations – I Can't Get Next to You
The Temptations – The Way You Do the Things You Do
The Temptations – You're Not an Ordinary Girl
The Third Time Around – Soon Everything is Gonna Be Alright
The Three Caps (AKA The Capitols) – Cool Jerk
The Toys – A Lover's Concerto
The Trammps – Hold Back the Night
The Trammps – Scrub-Board
The Trammps – Sixty Minute Man
The Upsetters – The Return of Django
The Velours – I'm Gonna Change
The Velvelettes – He Was Really Saying Something
The Velvelettes – Needle in a Haystack
The Velvelettes – These Things Will Keep Me Loving You
The Vel-Vets – I Got to Find Me Somebody
The Voices of East Harlem – Cashing In
The Watts 103rd Street Rhythm Band – The Joker
The Wombles – Remember You're a Womble
Thelma Houston – Don't Leave Me This Way
Timi Yuro – It'll Never be Over For Me
Titanic – Sultana
Tobi Legend – Time Will Pass You By
Today's People – S.O.S. (All We Need is Time for Love)
Tommy James and the Shondells – Mony Mony
Tommy Neal – Going to a Happening
Toni Basil – Breakaway
Tony Blackburn (released as 'Lenny Gamble' on the Casino Classics label) – I'll Do Anything
Tony Joe White – Polk Salad Annie
Train, Keep on Movin' – The Fifth Dimension
Troy Keyes – If I Had My Way
Van McCoy – Strings Sweet and Easy
Van McCoy – The Hustle
Velvet – Bet You If You Ask Around
Velvet Hammer – Happy
Vernon Garrett - Shine it On
Vicky Sue Robinson – Turn the Beat Around
Wall of Sound – Hang On
Wayne Fontana – Something Keeps Calling Me Back
Wayne Gibson – Under My Thumb

Wendy Rene – Bar-B-Q
Wigan's Chosen Few – Footsee
Wigan's Ovation – Per-so-nal-ly
Wigan's Ovation – Skiing in the Snow
Wigan's Ovation – Superlove
William Bell – Happy
Willie Mitchell – Secret Home
Willie Mitchell – That Driving Beat
Willie Tee – Walking Up a One Way Street
Wilson Pickett – 634-5789
Wilson Pickett – In the Midnight Hour
Wilson Pickett – Land of 1,000 Dances
Wilson Pickett – Mustang Sally
Wilson Pickett – Three Time Loser
Witches and the Warlock – Behind Locked Doors
Wombat – I'm Getting' on Life
Wynder K Frog – Green Door

Printed in Great Britain
by Amazon